SIMON T. BAILEY

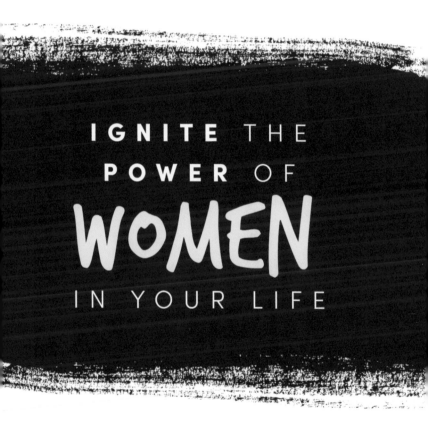

IGNITE THE
POWER OF
WOMEN
IN YOUR LIFE

[A GUIDE FOR MEN]

Printed in the United States of America
ISBN-13: 978-1-7325994-6-8

Collaborators:	Ellena Balkom and Jen Miller
Copy Editor:	Caroline Barthalomew
Proofreader:	Positively Proofed, Plano, TX
Design:	Kendra Cagle, 5 Lakes Design, Wolcott, NY
Credits:	Photographer: Victoria Angel Photography Location: Four Seasons Hotel Orlando

DEDICATION

This book is dedicated to my children:

Daniel, you shine so brightly; Madison, you are smart and an old soul; Ashley, you are a gifted artist; and Chelsey, you are one of the kindest human beings on the planet.

LOVE IS NOT JUST WHAT YOU SAY, IT IS WHAT YOU DO.

It's an action. There is so much I have neglected to tell you four, and this book is my love story to you. I love you enough to have written down my feelings and my failures, and I'm sharing them with you in the hope that you can know me more fully and perhaps live richer lives because of that.

TABLE OF CONTENTS

ACKNOWLEDGEMENTS

This book could not have been written without the encouragement of my wife, Jodi, my therapist, Anita Riggs, RN LMHC CAP, and my spiritual mentor for over 20 years, Dr. Mark Chironna.

Jodi knew I had been working on this book, but I decided without telling her that I wanted to put it on the shelf. It was just too personal and maybe not what the world wanted to read about. She turned to me after we heard a thought-provoking speaker at the Engage Summits meeting and said...

YOU HAVE TO FINISH YOUR BOOK!

Thank you for the push, Jodi!

Anita was introduced to me by my divorce attorney, who suggested that I seek professional help. There, I said it. Let me be frank; No man in his right mind wants to admit he can benefit from sitting on a sofa twice a month for an hour over an 18-month period talking with a therapist named Anita. Especially when she's a woman who has been practicing mental health and healing for almost 40 years and has more degrees than a thermostat! Nevertheless, I went. In our very first session, Anita said, "Whatever you don't deal with will eventually deal with you." Well, that wisdom started me on a path to become a proud MVP – Most Vulnerable Person. Thank you, Anita!

A man of impeccable character, Dr. Chironna has been a force for good in my life. Through the years, he and his wife, Ruth, have prayed for me, counseled me, and coached me. The most well-read man I've ever met, Mark knows philosophy, religion, psychology and European and African history. Thank you, Dr. Chironna and Ruth, for never giving up on me and for supporting my ideas!

I would also like to give a shout out to a woman named Arielle Ford to whom I was introduced by Kristine Carlson at a luncheon for the Association of Transformational Leadership – Southern California chapter. I explained to Arielle the idea for this book that day, and right then she took out an index card, wrote something on it, gave it to me and said: "This should be the title of your book." And she was right. Thank you, Arielle!

Calvin, my big brother, thank you for helping me during some of the darkest times in my life.

Robert, you've been my best friend since fourth grade, and here we are some 40 years later still rolling, laughing and channeling Crockett and Tubbs from *Miami Vice*. I am so proud of your sons – Jeremiah, the future MD, and Caleb, the future entrepreneur.

Finally, I would like to acknowledge the following women who have had a profound impact on my life and career: my mother, Mary Bailey; Rosa Stephens; Renee Bailey; Debbie Wilson; Dr. Johnetta Cole; Valerie Ferguson; Patricia Engfer; Janis Petrie; Hattie Hill; Michelle Mason; Amy Taylor; Mel Robbins; Rebecca Grinnals; Kathryn Arce; Carrie Wittman; Mary Kenny; Jamie O'Donnell; Ileana Gaskill; Merryl Brown; Jen Miller; Jan Miller; Shannon Marven; Laura Fitzgerald; Jayne Warrilow; Marley Majcher; Kathleen Bertrand; Phyllis Day; and my adopted sisters for over 30 years, Sonya Irby, Margarethia Bledsoe, Pam Pruitt and Julie Grubbs.

INTRODUCTION

Stuart Johnson, founder and CEO of **Success Partners,** asked me several years ago to host and emcee the company's Success Live program in Long Beach, CA. The night before the event was to start, the producers told me they also wanted me to fill a hole in the schedule by sharing a personal story. Well, that night, I barely slept a wink. I tossed and turned contemplating what I should share and how deep I should go. Late into the night, I pecked out a few words on my PC, then decided to delete them and go off script.

Here's the story I told that next day.

My daughter, Madison, came to me one afternoon and asked if we could talk. I said: *"Sure, how are you?"* But my body language must have said: *"I'm pretty busy here, Maddie, what could be so important?"* Reading that and not my empty words, she said: *"It's okay, Dad, I'll just see you later."*

That's when it hit me. I was emotionally unavailable to my own daughter. I had missed an important moment to be there for her, to be a tuned-in and loving father. As my then-wife Renee pointed out, I was giving the world my best, but giving my family the rest. I thought to myself, *"If I don't change my behavior, my daughter will end up marrying a jumper like me."* I was unintentionally also modeling detached, self-absorbed and uncaring behavior for my son. He was likely to do the same in his relationships.

I am happy to report that my short, candid talk moved many in the audience. I could tell as I recounted the story that people were sitting up, paying attention. But I wasn't ready for what happened next. Goalcast.com contacted **Success Partners** and got permission to edit my story from a 12-minute talk to three minutes and a few seconds. Well, that short clip about how one daughter made her father question everything he was doing was posted on Facebook and received 16,000 views in less than 24 hours.

As I'm writing this book, it has grown to...

 MORE THAN 90 MILLION VIEWS,

 GENERATED 6,000 COMMENTS,

 AND 233,746 SHARES.

It's been reshared on Instagram by Rapper/Actor **@David Banner**, Rapper TI **@troubleman31**, Beyonce's mom **@MsTina Lawson** and Author/Purpose Coach **@Jayshetty**. Basically, the video went viral.

The comments posted in the video feed really grabbed me by the throat and were from men and women all over the world. I'll share a few of them with you.

SHERRY WROTE:

"My children's father has always missed important events and milestones in his children's lives, who are now 13 and 11. Almost every birthday or special occasion, his response is, 'I gotta work.' He's already missed so many precious moments of their lives and has made no memories with them, although we are in the same town. He has taught them nothing. One day I hope he runs across this video and gets it."

ZAC SAID:

"I wish I could turn back time and not commute to be there with Donnie when he was small. Sometimes buying them everything means nothing if you're not physically there because of work."

DEEPAK WROTE:

"If I were to take this advice, I'll be feeding my kids only bread instead of steak. It's tough to find a balance in life within my family and career, especially living in a developing economy like mine where opportunities are only given to family members of people in power... even having a post-graduate degree didn't help."

Jason said:

"*I cry every day for what I did wrong. It's true. I focused on my career. I wanted the best for everyone. In the end, I lost my family because they didn't have to want for anything. Now all I want is my family. It's gone. Ugh.*"

You can see that the video struck a chord, or rang a few bells, I should say.

Here's the truth:

People all over the globe, particularly men, are struggling with being both the breadwinner for the family and a present parent and partner.

It made me think, maybe it's time to delve deeper into this conundrum. Maybe we need some insights, some guidelines for how to respond with love, how to listen on a truly deep level. How can we men best work and co-parent with the women in our lives? How can we help each other? How do we, as men, model vulnerable behavior and help propel the women in our lives to reach their full potential? How do we ignite the power within them and allow that power to, in turn, empower us?

It's taken me three years to write this book – ten different drafts, three title changes, untold sleepless nights. Any of you who've read my previous work, listened to me as a keynote speaker, watched one of my podcasts or followed me on social media knows that this content is a total departure for me. It's the hardest book I've ever written: It's intimate and personal and I've always been closed up and private. It has come from the harsh realization that I needed to change – shed the skin of the lost, lonely, insecure man I was – drop the mask of the great pretender and become a fully feeling and wholly vulnerable person. It has come from 18 months of intense therapy. It has come from facing my painful past and my many failures, my divorce.

I wrote this guide to pass on the costly, crucial and precious lessons I've learned the hard way, to help men figure out how to best be in a healthy relationship with women, to aid us males in understanding that we are better if we know how to light the infinite and imminent spark in women so they can live on fire and warm us in the process.

I wrote this book for women, too, so they can appreciate how men think, understand how to encourage the men in their lives and confirm what they intuitively know about men by giving them context and real information. I want women to see why it's difficult, but certainly not impossible, for men to become the vulnerable people they need us to be.

Probably, I could have written this book without baring my soul. It could have been like my other books – based on data, research and executive know-how, meant to motivate and stimulate people professionally. After all, I've coached and mentored dozens of women from all over the globe. These were women in CEO roles, women who were starting businesses, and many who achieved seven-figure salaries. Beyond that, over the past 30 years, I've observed and listened to thousands of women, both personally and professionally. So, I could have written what I knew, or what I thought I knew in this case, and I just might have pulled it off.

But that would have been me before I hit rock bottom. That would have been me before I realized that rising up in the world doesn't mean living in a 6,000-square-foot house in a million-dollar neighborhood with custom furniture and drapes, tooling around in a Mercedes-Benz and a Range Rover and flying my entire family to Maui for ten days at a time. That would have been me before I realized that my wife and I didn't cherish each other, that we hadn't for years, that for 25 years we had been going through the motions acting like the picture-perfect family when, in fact, we were coming apart at the seams. That would have been me before I realized I was a hamster in a cage on a treadmill – working, always working to pay the bills, stay afloat, but never really enjoying my life or spending time with our children. That would have been me before I saw that we had run through our savings, and I had nothing to show for twelve years of work.

That would have been me before therapy, before becoming an MVP, Most Vulnerable Person.

No, this book called for candor and sensitivity, for tender confessions and ugly truths. So, what you're getting here is real, solid information and advice gleaned over many years, as well as real, solid, emotional honesty — let's call it the secret sauce, the sole (or soul) ingredient that makes the whole pot of soup more delicious.

AND IT IS MY FERVENT WISH THAT YOU WILL BE ABLE TO TASTE THE DIFFERENCE.

CHAPTER ONE

THE **AGE** OF THE WOMAN

If you don't know it by now, I'm here to tell you that we've entered the Age of the Woman.

I'm actually writing this portion of the book in London, England, while I'm in a two-week, self-imposed quarantine before traveling to Milan, Italy. I am a stone's throw away from the Tower of London, the Royal Mint and the Bank of England. Maybe from Queen Elizabeth herself. Do you want to talk about an incredibly strong woman? She's been her country's longest-serving monarch, and her influence reverberates around the world. She's been a shining example of the female work ethic for decades.

WE MEN KNOW THAT
→POWERFUL WOMEN←
HAVE EXISTED SINCE THE DAWN OF HISTORY.

Queens come to mind – Cleopatra, Catherine the Great, Victoria and Elizabeth I. Then there are the female warriors like Joan of Arc. More recently, countless females have changed the world for the better. Right off the bat, I'm thinking Ruth Bader Ginsburg, Eleanor Roosevelt, Mother Teresa, Rosa Parks, Michelle Obama and the three women (Katherine Johnson, Dorothy Vaughan and Mary Jackson) who were the brilliance behind astronaut John Glenn's Friendship 7 mission to orbit the earth – a feat that restored faith in the nation's space program.

So, female strength, intelligence and leadership are certainly nothing new. So, why am I saying that now is the Age of the Woman?

Because around the globe it's becoming plain that when women have a seat at the table, when they are put in leadership roles in government and corporations, when women are treated as equals, the world is a safer and better place.

An article dated September 11, 2021, in The Economist titled *"Why nations that fail women fail,"* quotes Hillary Clinton from a decade ago: *The subjugation of women is... a threat to the common security of our world.*

The article further states:

SOCIETIES THAT OPPRESS WOMEN ARE FAR MORE LIKELY TO BE VIOLENT AND UNSTABLE.

When peace talks include women, the accord lasts longer, the article claims, partly due to a woman's inclination to compromise.

Research tells us that women control 20 trillion dollars' worth of spending globally. Research says that when women are on the boards of corporations or have senior executive roles, those companies experience a positive bottom line and amazing profitability.

McKinsey + Company's study of one thousand companies in twelve countries found that organizations in the top 25 percent when it comes to gender diversity among executive leadership teams were more likely to outperform by 21 percent on profitability and 27 percent on value creation (McKinsey, "Delivering Through Diversity," 2018).

According to an article in *U.S. News and World Report* by Allyson Bear and Roselle Agner, "Countries with women who are head of state such as Denmark, Finland, Iceland, New Zealand, Germany and Slovakia have been internationally recognized for the effectiveness of their response to the pandemic. These women leaders were proactive in responding to the threat of the virus, implementing social distancing restrictions early, seeking expert advice to inform health strategies and unifying the country around a comprehensive response with transparent and compassionate communication."

The article goes on to say, *"A Harvard Business School study has shown women leaders have a measurable impact on the bottom line, with venture capital firms that hired more female partners showing increased profitability. The presence of women leaders in national, local and community level governance leads to an increase in policy making that advances rights, promotes equality and improves quality of life for those overlooked in society"* (U.S. News & World Report, "Why More Countries Need Female Leaders," March 8, 2021).

The moment when men who call themselves leaders respect, honor and protect women is when they will experience innovative breakthroughs and thrive instead of holding on by a thread or merely getting by. The United Nation's 17 Sustainable Development Goals (SDGs) to transform our world within the next decade are only possible if there is a woman at the table leading or co-leading the conversation.

Another interesting trend is that more women are now earning college degrees than men. New York University professor Scott Galloway gives us the facts in one of his podcasts. In 1970, he says, 59 percent of U.S. college students were men. That number has now decreased to 40 percent. American colleges receive 35 percent more applications from females than males. If the trend continues, Galloway points out, women will earn twice as many college degrees as men.

He goes on to conclude that we may be creating an underclass in this country – an underclass called men (Prof G Media, Chart of the Week, September, 22, 2021).

So WHAT DOES THAT MEAN FOR US MALES?

Who will these women marry if men are falling behind and not keeping up intellectually?

Women also will more than likely start elbowing men out of white-collar jobs and start businesses at a record clip ahead of men.

WAKE UP AND READ THE TEA LEAVES, GENTLEMEN!

Women are a force to be reckoned with, and we need them now more than ever, **MORE THAN WE KNOW.**

Why is it that we men are sometimes clueless, like we walk around on eggshells, not knowing what to say, afraid we're going to say the wrong thing, afraid our words will be taken out of context? Why are we afraid to engage in deeper conversations with and about women?

The reason, I believe, that sometimes men marginalize, miscommunicate with and are misinformed about women is because somewhere along the way another man told us we need to change women, that we need to control them. Really? You're kidding, right? How's that working out for you right now, huh?

THE REALITY IS THAT WOMEN DON'T NEED TO BE CONTROLLED, THEY NEED TO BE UNDERSTOOD.

Women want to have a conversation that goes three miles deep, not just small, surface talk. I learned that very quickly one Monday morning when my daughter, Madison, asked me if she could drive to school and have me sit in the passenger seat. I said something like: *"Sure, okay, you've got your learner's permit and are working on getting your driver's license."*

Well, about halfway to school, Madison asked: *"Dad, how am I doing?"*

Being the emotionally clueless dad, I said: *"You're doing fine."*

When we got to school and she got out, I hugged her, kissed her on the forehead and she was off. As I was driving away, it dawned on me that I had just missed an opportunity to connect with my daughter. I had said her driving was fine instead of taking the time to go deeper and give her at least three reasons why her driving was fine.

I know, I know, I did it again. I was elsewhere when my daughter needed me to be with her, in the moment. I'm a slow learner, okay?

I believe there needs to be a greater conversation with men about how we begin to awaken and think about how we treat women, how we're showing up in relationships with them.

Recently, I was talking to a group of CEOs and told them this:

"A MAN, A NATION, A SOCIETY AND A CORPORATION WILL NOT UNLEASH ITS POTENTIAL UNTIL IT DOES RIGHT BY WOMEN."

Guys, it took me 20 years to figure this out. Just like understanding that I needed to be present for Madison, it took me a minute. Let's just say that I was in the bottom half of the class that made the top half of the class possible.

I invited those CEOs to consider making a commitment to begin to honor and respect women, not because it's the right thing to do but because they want to do it. I encouraged them to create pathways whereby women could rise from staff roles to line roles to CEO roles if they wanted to, to move from non-management into management because they are competent.

Oh, and by the way, those of you ladies who are in senior leadership positions, don't forget your sisters. Don't elbow them out. Advise them, assist them and communicate ways they can climb the corporate ladder.

WHY DO WE NEED WOMEN NOW
MORE THAN EVER
AND MORE THAN WE KNOW?

I'LL GIVE YOU THREE GOOD REASONS.

1. **Women have amazing intelligence.** In fact, I'll go out on a limb here and tell you that a woman's brain is bigger than a man's. That's right, I said it. That doesn't make

men any less in comparison to women, it's just that we need to hear them, respect what they have to say and take them seriously. A woman's intelligence (WI) is faster than artificial intelligence (AI). So, forget AI, we need to say WI! A woman can remember the date, the time, the location, who said what, who had what on, what didn't happen and what was the tone regarding a specific occurrence in a nanosecond. Sadly, in life and in our society, according to Mike Murdock, prolific author and host of the School of Wisdom, a woman's particular intelligence is tolerated instead of celebrated. Let's change that now!

2. **Women have intuition, a sixth sense or a gut knowledge about something long before men ever get it.** In an Op-Ed piece for the *New York Times*, David Brooks wrote that for many years, scientists have focused on thinking; but going forward they're focusing on thinking that happens not just in the brain but in the gut. In fact, I will never forget a time when I signed a business deal that I was all gung-ho about. I had looked at the numbers and thought it was awesome. I told my then-wife about the deal and she asked me to introduce her to my new business associates. I thought to myself: "Woman, you don't know what I know. This is going to be great." Nevertheless, she and I had lunch with them, and afterward she said: "Simon, I don't know what type of deal you signed with them, but I would strongly encourage you to get out of it." I questioned why. She said, "There is just something off about them. I can't put my finger on it, but I don't think you need to be in business with them. I don't trust them." Turns out she was spot on. I ended up having to sue these business partners to get out of an agreement that could have been avoided if I'd leaned into her intuitive advice.

3. **Women have a natural ability to innovate.** Ask a woman a question and she'll give you a dissertation. Give a woman a vision and she'll give you strategies and tactics. Hand a woman a problem and she'll offer options that will blow you away.

I can't get anywhere by thinking that I am a manly man, the keeper of the castle, or as "Macho Man" Randy Savage said, the tower of power. No, that dog just won't hunt anymore.

I invite you men to stand up and recognize that the only way for us to get into the future is to let the women in our lives tell us the truth. Believe me, a woman won't tell you everything she knows all at once. If she told you all she knows, you'd blow a circuit in your brains, my friends. No, she'll tell you what you need to know, what you can handle, to become all you can possibly be, one teaspoon at a time.

WE MALES NEED TO SHIFT - SEE HOW I FIT TOMORROW.

Nations, corporations, communities and societies have to shift. We have to ask how we can co-exist and co-create, how we can move from "me" to "we." Because I need you and you need me. Because I'll say it again; Men need women.

So, join me on this journey if you will, this mission to let every man in on the great truth that women are the sparks. We can no longer tell a woman; we must ask her. We should no longer try to merely communicate with a woman; we should also try to connect with her. It's true that when we light the sparks of a woman's brilliance, it opens up the brilliance in us.

CHAPTER TWO

TELL **HER** THE TRUTH

Lennox and Deanna, my dear friends, heard that I was soon to be a deer-in-the-headlights divorcee. They suggested I take part in a Landmark Forum, a three-day, intensive session designed to produce positive and permanent changes that lead to healthier relationships, greater confidence and increased enjoyment of life. I had not heard of this organization, but I trusted my friends and went to Washington, D.C., to attend. I'm forever grateful that I did. What I heard and learned that weekend furthered and deepened my break-through that started with my therapist, Anita Riggs. It was an experience I'll never forget for the rest of my life.

The facilitator challenged us, the attendees, to come totally clean with the important people in our lives. One of our assignments was to write a letter to someone we needed to be totally honest with.

My letter was to my ex-wife, Renee, the mother of my two children who gave me 25 years of her life.

HERE'S THE GIST OF WHAT I WROTE.

"The truth is, I wasn't happy with myself, so I couldn't be happy in our marriage. I pretended a lot. I was really disinterested and half-hearted. Things I should have been passionate about, I was just checking off a list. I blamed you for so many things, including our financial situation, when it was my stubborn desire to do it my way that got us in a bind.

"While I was fooling the outside world into believing I had the perfect life and marriage, I was actually using my vows to hide my desperate need to be mothered and rescued. My pretense, arrogance and air of perfection *were also concealing the fact that I felt like a fraud. I was afraid to let anyone get to know me. I wasn't listening to you like I should have; instead, I was all the way shut down. My way of coping with anxiety, fear, stress and worry was to close down."*

I ended the letter with an apology:

"My inauthentic way of being has cost us dearly and negatively impacted our family. I am sorry for not being completely honest with you. I am sorry and I hope you can forgive me for the pain I have caused you and our children. Now, as we go our separate ways, my only hope is that we can become friends and raise our two awesome children together."

I STILL CHOKE UP
WHEN I READ BACK OVER THESE WORDS.

It is still so painful to come face-to-face with the harm I have caused and the self-doubt that allowed me to act insensitively and callously. But the letter was cathartic for me – it was me ripping off the mask of always being on and acting like I was the smartest person in the room when, in fact, I was often clueless. Telling the truth about myself was both liberating and cleansing. I believed, for the first time, that everything was going to be okay for us.

Telling the truth about myself made me want to rip off more layers and understand why I was always running from my past, as my therapist put it.

Truth is, I was ashamed of my past – of being born into a poor family, of growing up in a city where the options for young Black men were few, or so I thought.

When I was 11 years old, a man led me down a dark staircase in a neighbor's house and attempted to sexually abuse me.

I didn't tell anyone.

When I was 14, I was failing in school. About that time in my life, I was playing on a basketball court across the street from my house and a young guy told me I was as Black as tar and so ugly. I ran home, grabbed the keys to my mom's car, went into the garage and closed the door behind me. I got into the car and started the ignition, trying to take my life. But, thankfully, something stopped me, something breathed "Don't do it." I believe it was God.

When I was 15, my parents moved me to another school, hoping I would finish. And I did, thank goodness.

Later, I ran from my life in Atlanta to Florida and into a marriage with no pre-marital counseling, no financial safety net and minimal work skills.

OVER THE PAST 35 YEARS, I'VE FALLEN FLAT ON MY FACE MANY TIMES.

I know now that I have struggled with low self-esteem and low self-worth all of my life. I know now that I didn't like or love myself. And I sure didn't know how to be in a relationship with another person, let alone a woman.

The lesson here is clear: We men need to deal with our own insecurities honestly and with the disappointing pasts we are running from. We men need to do some serious soul searching. We need to work on understanding why we do the things we do, why we close up and refuse to communicate before we can expect to have a meaningful and rich relationship with a woman, much less encourage her to be her best self, to ignite her uniquely feminine power so she can love us as we want to be loved.

REFLECTION

When you read the summary of my letter to my ex-wife, what resonated with you as you thought about where you are right now, whether single, between relationships, happy being alone, married, engaged, divorced or widowed?

Are you willing to be that honest with yourself and others?

Until you are, you'll always have a mask on, and no one will get to know the real you.

⇒RECOMMENDATION⇐

 ## SINGLE

Constantly work on yourself by actively participating in personal growth workshops that invite you to look in the mirror and become a better human being. Find a community of individuals who challenge you. They can point the mirror right at you and tell you the truth.

 ## BETWEEN RELATIONSHIPS

What did you learn from the last one? How will you show up differently and better in the next one? Are you looking for a relationship to save you? If so, stop!

 ## MARRIED

Are you ready to have a real conversation with your spouse? Or, are you planning to continue to sweep things under the rug as if there is no problem? Well, if you are, I can promise you that you may have sex, but you will never make love or move into deeper in-ti-ma-cy (Into Me See). I strongly encourage you to see a professional therapist to help you and your spouse stay fine-tuned.

ENGAGED

A therapist once told me that a couple looking to marry needs to have a minimum of 50 to 100 hours of communication before they do. The ability to listen without judgment is crucial to understanding who this person is at the core. I highly suggest you consider pre-marital counseling before taking the leap.

DIVORCED

You are HERE. That's what the map at the mall would tell you. Realize that divorce has happened and that the greatest gift you can give yourself is to breathe. Don't beat yourself up, and stop going over and over what happened to get you where you are. Know that you will have memories of the good times and the bad times that will haunt you like sad ghosts. Remember, breathe!

[CHAPTER THREE]

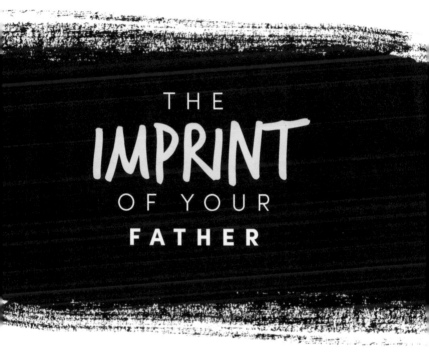

THE IMPRINT OF YOUR FATHER

Confession time... I miss my father. Not too long ago, I was on a flight from Mexico back to the U.S. and I found I couldn't stop crying. Thank God I was in a window seat, turning my head away from my seatmate so he wouldn't think I was a wuss. Oh well, so what, I missed my father. I wished he were still alive so we could go on a long car ride on the QEW (the major highway that runs from Buffalo to Toronto) and talk like we used to.

WHY DID ALL OF THAT EMOTION HIT ME ALL OF A SUDDEN AT 30,000  FEET?

I had just been watching George H.W. Bush's funeral from the television in my hotel room, and I had had a visceral reaction to son George W. Bush's heartfelt eulogy. In it, Bush emphasized what a loyal friend his father had been, what a family man and a servant leader he was. He said that everything he and his brothers had accomplished and become were because of the example his father had set. He choked up as he recalled his father's final words to him: *"Son, I love you."*

I hate to admit it (although therapy has made it a bit easier), but there was a time I didn't tell my children I loved them. My then-wife and their mother, Renee, brought that sad fact up to me once, and my response was that my father had never said it to me. Renee cut her eyes at me and said: "Well, you may want to do something about it sooner rather than later."

HMMM...ALL THIS WHILE I THOUGHT I WORE THE PANTS IN THE FAMILY.

Maybe, but if so, she was definitely the belt that held those pants up.

So, I called my father and asked why he had never told me he loved me. He answered: *"I might not have said it, but I put food on the table, clothes on your back and a roof over your head. That was my way of saying I love you."*

I persisted: *"But, Dad, you never said it."*

Then, he told me a story I'll never forget. When he was eight years old growing up in Kingston, Jamaica, he said, his father died, and since he was the oldest sibling, he had to drop out of school to seek some form of income for the family. *"Simon,"* he said, *"I couldn't give you what I didn't receive. I couldn't be someone I wasn't, and I couldn't do what hadn't been done for me. However, I want you to know that I love you and believe in you."*

Well, those words ricocheted off the walls of my hungry soul, a soul that had been starving for affirmation from the man who was responsible for my existence. His words were an emotional tattoo inked onto my heart that will never be erased. I so needed to hear that I mattered to him, that he saw me. It was then that I turned to my children, Daniel and Madison, and told them I loved them, that I was grateful to and for them, that I was sorry I hadn't told them before. In their eyes I could see joy and relief, and I knew then and there the mighty power that a father wields, a power that can either light someone else's fire or extinguish it totally.

Where are you men with this?

How is or was your relationship with your father? Was he there for you? What kind of imprint did he leave on you?

God knows fathers aren't perfect, far from it. Regardless of what your father did wrong, I invite you to forgive him and let it go if you can. If you can't, get help, talk to someone about it. I invite you to forgive for your own benefit, so you don't continue to self-sabotage relationships, business opportunities and your own health and happiness. Believe me, I know. I filled my father void with spending precious time acquiring things, shiny toys that gave me a false and fleeting pleasure. I filled it by staying busy, anything to take my attention away from my hurt.

I'M ASKING YOU, IMPLORING YOU, TO HEAL THE FATHER WOUND.

⇒RECOMMENDATION⇐

Tell your father how you feel about your relationship with him. Talk honestly without blaming him. He did the best he could. Forgive him for any hurt he may have caused, and decide to communicate openly from now on. If you can't bring yourself to speak to him, write a letter. Writing can be very therapeutic and can heal many wounds. However you say it, put your emotions out there. Only then can you move on, free yourself from the past and live your life unburdened.

While we're at it, forgive your mother for what she did or didn't do. She had the important job; she carried you for nine months and brought you into this world. Thank God for mothers! Forgive your wife, spouse, baby or boo for any hurt she may have caused you. Forgive your siblings, too. That's right. Some of you reading this right now only talk to your brothers and sisters on holidays, birthdays or if there has been a death in the family. You can do better, and you know it. Forgive and forget!

**After that, thank them for what they did right,
for the specific lessons they taught you.**

In my case, my father, Reginald Bailey, a totally self-made man who picked oranges and apples to earn money to feed his family and taught himself to read by using the Bible, left me with three important lessons:

1. **The best hand to feed you is at the end of your own wrist.** Never underestimate the value and power of a strong work ethic. Because of this advice, I have gotten up between 4 and 5 a.m. every single day, because I know nothing is going to fall out of the sky for me unless I get up and make it happen.

2. **Love and respect have no color.**

3. **Love your mother, respect her and take care of her as I have done.**

My father was a good man and I miss him terribly. Still, I had to do some work to understand my mixed feelings about him, work that I encourage you to do as well.

I know that everything I've talked about here may seem oversimplified. You might be saying: "Simon, it's easy for you to say, but you don't know my situation." You're right. I don't. I'm not a licensed therapist. Perhaps you need to seek one out. I highly recommend professional help.

Here's the bottom line:

You cannot go brightly into the future, much less enjoy a mutually loving relationship with a woman, until you deal with your issues. I think it may start with examining your father's imprint.

As an aside, find out about the relationship the woman you are seriously dating has with her father. The very first man she ever loved is her Dad; the very first man who represented what it means to be a man is her Dad; the one who showed her how a man treats a woman is her Dad. You need to know her psychological framework and her perception of her father because it will show up in your relationship.

After realizing how powerful a father's words can be, I decided to turn Father's Day around. Usually, it's the day children show their appreciation and give their fathers gifts. But I wanted my children to know what a gift they are to me, so I started writing letters to them. Here is one of the letters I wrote to my children on Father's Day. I hope you'll find it raw and real and that it helps you see some of what I've learned – both good and bad – from being a father.

Daniel and Madison,

Both of you have grown into fine young adults. I cannot believe, Daniel, that you've finished your first year of college, and Madison, you're about to graduate from high school and enter college.

I remember so many people telling me to enjoy every moment with you before you transition to the next stage of your life. I thought they were just kidding, but as time keeps on slippin', slippin', slippin' into the future, as the Steve Miller band sang, they were right.

I realize that one day you will have children of your own, so it's imperative that I be transparent with you.

I know that I often used work and travel or scheduled meetings as an excuse for not being at home. Please for-

give me for being emotionally unavailable to your mother, thus making myself emotionally disconnected to you. I am your Dad, and I was wrong. I am sorry.

Somehow, despite my shortcomings, both of you have found your own resilience and are two of my favorite people in the world. You are courteous, kind, respectful, nice, consistent, hardworking and smart like your mother.

Daniel – you've turned out to be a bright young man with the heart of God. Madison – you are a beautiful young lady who is an emerging global leader with a taste for the finer things in life.

I JUST WANT TO TAKE A MOMENT TO HELP YOU APPLY SOME MENTAL FLOSS TO YOUR THINKING:

- *Relationships are the currency of the future. Strive to build rapport with people, not because of what they can do for you but what you can do for them.*

- *The world doesn't owe you anything. Go to work. Give more than is required for what you are paid to do and watch what happens.*

- *Ask for help. Sometimes God puts people in your path to help you along the way.*

- *Feed the poor.*

- *Be obsessed with having a spirit of excellence. Being average is not an option. That's not what you are or what our family stands for.*

- *Be on time. That means a minimum of 15 minutes prior to the scheduled time.*

This Father's Day, I wanted to share with you some of what I've learned from being your father. Thank you for being the greatest teachers and mentors I will ever have.

I love you both.

Love,
Your Dad

If you're a father, a father-to-be or struggling with the idea of having children, I can offer you three ways to make a difference in your children's lives and leave them a lasting legacy:

- **One of my favorite things to do is send letters and postcards to my children from wherever I am in the world.** I truly believe that in the future my children will see these correspondences as tangible proof that I loved them and that they were always forefront in my thoughts.

- **Record a video for your grandchildren – yes, even if they don't exist yet.** Tell them how old you are, where you are in your life, share your thoughts, hopes and dreams and the possibilities you see for them.

- **Prepare your children financially for the future, for adulthood.** Do your best to provide for your children's education. Teach them early about spending wisely and saving. Even if your financial means are limited, your ability to create an impact is not.

Renee and I were adamant about financially supporting our children's college education. (I didn't want them contributing to our country's trillion-dollar student loan debt.) But we have also tried not to enable them. When they were in college, I gave them 45-days' notice before they became responsible for paying for their own phone bills. Within a week, both of them had found part-time jobs. And that's just the start. Next up is asking them to pay for their car insurance, rent and any advanced degrees they may go for. The lessons we are imparting are simple: Life is tough but so are you. Figure it out.

[CHAPTER FOUR]

CARITAS
TRANSFORMATION

At one of the lowest points in my personal life during the COVID-19 pandemic, I was invited to give a virtual presentation to the top 1,500 leaders of Stanford Healthcare, the teaching hospital for Stanford University School of Medicine. Having found me through a Google search, they wanted me to share my insights on how to lead in times of chaos and change.

I WAS IMMEDIATELY ANXIOUS.

What in the world could I share with these fine medical minds? And how in the world could I hope to impress them when I had to follow superstar Tom Rath, author of several bestselling books on leadership and well-being and a regular guest lecturer at the University of Pennsylvania?

Well, I worked on that presentation for weeks because I didn't want to make a fool of myself. I shared my best thinking and anchored it in research. I spoke about why and how it's important to take care of yourself first, about how to deal with unforeseen events. I attempted to give them tangible tools that would help them connect with their team members. Finally, I spoke about how to hear, heal and help in response to George Floyd's murder.

My hard work had an unexpected payoff. I received over a dozen positive messages via LinkedIn from attendees. One that stuck out was from Grissel Hernandez, PhD, MPH, RN and executive director of the Center for Education & Professional Development. She suggested I explore the work of a woman named Dr. Jean Watson. Grissel told me that Dr. Watson, "the Lady Gaga of nursing," was a 40-year scholar in the field of what's called Caring Science and the Human Caring Theory. This practice goes beyond merely using science to heal patients, but teaches the moral, ethical and philosophical importance of truly caring for humankind and is being taught throughout the healthcare system. Unbeknownst to me, I had used caring science language in my presentation, and that's why Grissel invited me to get to know Dr. Watson and her work, and then introduced me to her.

I was so taken by Dr. Watson's aura and energy that I decided to enroll in a six-month caring science program called Caritas Coaching Education Program, or CCEP for short. (Caritas is a Latin word that means charity or Christian love of humanity.) I had no idea what I was getting myself into. I just wanted certification in an executive coaching program that was substantive and research based. Little did I know that immersing myself into this learning journey with thirty-nine medical professionals was the precise prescription I needed to make sense of the havoc the pandemic was wreaking on my soul.

The first concept I learned was to embrace a new way of being. Instead of feeling as if I needed to do more, I needed to be more. I needed to be more to myself. The way to accomplish this, I learned, is through centering. Okay, I know what you're thinking... is this some '60s psychobabble that sounds cool but has no real meaning? I thought the same thing—that is, until I really started using the concept, which is actually just a breathing and meditation exercise. Centering has become a total game changer for me. See, I was keeping so much inside, so much hidden deep within. Centering helped me exhale all of that so I could then inhale new possibilities.

Caritas and Caring Science taught me that before I can help anyone else, I must look at myself through a spiritual lens and practice self-love, self-care and compassion. I was able, through the Caritas training, to stop living in my head and tap into heart-centered intelligence. I was able to open up and communicate from a deeper place. I now have the framework to hold myself accountable and look for ways to stay open and serve the least, the last and the lost.

In Dr. Watson's words: "...in working from the radiance of the heart in this way, we are attuning to Universal Love. When we shift from fear or head to heart and begin to re-pattern our lives/energy fields, it affects our entire life... Further, as people change at the individual level, they see others differently, as teachers, or loving helpers, not as adversaries, enemies, or competitors" (Watson's book, *Caring Science as Sacred Science*).

I'd like to share four of the practices that Caring Science insists we use in our daily lives and how they have affected my life and relationships:

FORGIVENESS

One of the greatest challenges of my life over the past 30 years has been my relationship with my mother, who is now 81. When I was eight, I remember telling her that I was going to one day be wealthy enough to take care of her and my father. Well, to this day I'll never forget her response. She rolled her eyes, and in a discouraging tone she said, "You have big dreams, son." I felt like I'd been slapped. I internalized that hurt and carried it around inside for decades. And all that time I loved my mom at arm's length. I would do the perfunctory work of calling her every Sunday to check on her, and we'd talk for five or ten minutes. She would ask about the grandchildren, and we would end the call with, "I love you." But it was very mechanical and rote. There was no heart or deep connection in those conversations.

Caritas taught me it was finally time to forgive her. So, I asked my mom to forgive me for harboring resentment toward her all these years. Of course, she did. And she asked me to forgive her for what she so carelessly said those many years ago. Now, we're good, mom and me, but we wasted so much valuable time. My stubbornness wasn't protecting me, it was actually hurting me... As Dr. Watson says in her book, *Caring Science as Sacred Science:* "Somewhere along the way we learned to be resentful, angry and retaliatory toward others whom we felt harmed us in some way, but in harboring those feelings for others we hold those feelings against ourselves."

GRATITUDE

During the pandemic, the bottom fell out of my business. I didn't know how I was going to survive. At some point, I almost gave up and closed myself off from the world. I started binging on Netflix, carbs and sugar. Emotionally and mentally, I pulled the covers of disappointment over my head, waiting for it to all go away.

But Dr. Watson's words kept echoing in my head: "When we engage actively in re-patterning our consciousness, reconnecting us with God, and in doing so we are not only sustaining our own individual humanity, but humanity collectively."

I then thought about a song by gospel singer Walter Hawkins called "Thank You." I started singing the words: *I wanna say thank you for all you've done for me. Thank you for your power. Thank you for your protection. Thank you for your love.*

Practicing gratefulness in one of my darkest hours got me out of bed, off the couch and back into the world. Again from Dr. Watson's book: "In giving gratitude, we open ourselves to new energy and life force, releasing negative attachments which prevent us from honoring, experiencing all of life as a blessing and a teacher."

SURRENDERING

About a year ago, my daughter, Madison, told me that she and her college roommate had purchased tickets at $200 each to see Harry Styles, formerly with the band One Direction. The girls were counting the days until the concert, which had been re-scheduled three times due to the COVID crisis.

Well, a week or so before the concert, she told me she had several papers due and tests coming up. The helicopter dad in me was worried. Yes, I was really concerned. Her college costs were almost $60,000 per year and there was a long waiting list of young men and women who wanted to attend the school. Frankly, I didn't think she had time to go. Plus, there were going to be thousands of people at that concert. Were they vaccinated or not? Would she catch COVID-19? Who was going to be driving? What shenanigans might happen before or after the concert? Would she call me when she was safely back in her dorm room?

Yes, I was aware that I had dropped the ball when I was married to her mom. I hadn't been that in-volved in her life really. Was I now overcompensat-ing because I felt guilty? Was I still trying to hold onto Madison as if she were that 10-year-old girl I took to the American Girl store in Chicago? My head told me that she was 19, a responsible young lady with a good set of values. But my huge need to be in con-trol was getting the better of me.

As fate would have it, I was having lunch with my friend Patrick the day of the concert. He shared with me that his daughter was dying to go to the concert, too, but that tickets had gone up to $1,000 each. I couldn't believe it! I had, unwisely, just watched the movie *Taken*, about a CIA operative (Liam Neeson) who is tracking down his teenage daughter and her best friend who'd been kidnapped by Albanian human traffickers. I called Madison and was trying hard not to freak out about her safety, not to transfer my fear onto her.

She sounded happy, kind of grown up. It was at that moment that I realized I needed to surrender, to let her go. It was time for me to let her live her life, trust she had a level head on her shoulders and would make good decisions.

I didn't hear from her that night, so I sent her a text the next morning asking if she'd had fun. Of course, my real reason was to make sure she was safe and okay. She answered by sending me photos and videos of her roommate and her enjoying themselves to the max. I could hear such excitement in her voice, and I realized it was time to wake up, grow up and let go. Surrender.

Dr. Watson says: "[It is] in letting go of ego-sense of control and our efforts to make something happen, that we witness new possibilities unfolding right in front of us. When we fixate on making, or trying to make, every effort to fix something that is wrong and does not conform to the way we think things should be, we create more pain and suffering in our lives" (*Caring Science as Sacred Science*).

Boy, did that hit home. A recurring theme in my life, I realized in therapy, is a big need to be in control and to be right. Now I know it, and I'm really working hard to change that.

 ## COMPASSIONATE HUMAN SERVICE

Here's one last quote from Dr. Watson: "It is in this sense that we surrender ourself to a higher/deeper purpose to serve outside of our ego self, whereby we may be instruments through which caring is radiated from self to other, contributing to a healing in the midst of daily life" (*Caring Science as Sacred Science*).

A few years ago, I was invited by Compassion International, a Christian organization that sponsors children living in poverty-stricken areas of the world, to travel to the Dominican Republic on a mission trip. I'm not sure why I agreed to go, but I'm so glad I did. I ended up sponsoring two children: Anderson, 9, and Celestine, 10. Every month, along with countless other individuals, I make a small donation that ensures these children have food, shelter and a decent education.

Though the Caritas program transformed me in ways I am forever grateful for, I'm not recommending you enroll in order to live more compassionately. I hope I've given you some insight and direction in this chapter so you can understand how to get to a place where you can treat yourself, your wife, mother, daughter and anyone else in your life with the utmost care and love. Work on yourself first, get centered, then practice the four heart-focused developmental tasks as much as you possibly can so you can be lit from within and thereby stoke the fire in others.

RECOMMENDATION

Are you ready to practice forgiveness?

If so, take out a sheet of paper and write a letter to yourself and anyone else you need to forgive. No, I'm not asking you to send the letter but to just get it all out of your system.

When you hear the word "gratitude," what do you think about? What will you do to be more grateful in your life? Write it down.

WHAT IS ONE ACTION STEP YOU CAN TAKE TO SURRENDER AND LET GO?

What are you already doing to make a difference in the lives of others? How can you be more compassionate to the women in your life?

ONLINE DATING
—THE POWER OF THE SWIPE

After my divorce, my therapist, Anita, urged me emphatically not to start dating for at least a year. I asked why. She said that of the men who remarry within two years of getting divorced, 75 percent of them end up divorced again. She went on to say that after 12 months of therapy I should be a new man.

I decided to go on dates anyway. After having been married for 25 years, I didn't want to be alone. My plush, king-size bed felt cold, empty and uninviting. I was lonely.

So, I purchased several subscriptions to dating websites.

You name the site, and my picture (most were taken during my free-wheeling, so-called glory days of yore) would be on it – me playing with a dog, riding a camel in Abu Dhabi, looking super cool in Tel Aviv and having a blast in Australia.

NO ONE TOLD ME ONLINE DATING IS A FULL-TIME JOB OR THAT IT TAKES HOURS TO SCOUR THE INTERNET FOR A SUITABLE POTENTIAL MATE.

So, I solicited input from my cousin Deborah, who is like an older sister to me. (She's the same one who let me take a sip or two of alcohol at her house and dance to soul music when my ultra-religious, sanctified, Holy Ghost-filled parents weren't around. I thought then those were the best years ever!). Deborah suggested I form an unofficial board of advisers and seek help from them. I did just that. My board included Carrie, my BFF from my days working at Disney who stuck by me until the day I quit. Also on the team were Sonya,

Margarethia and Julie, my adopted sisters, as well as Jen, a dear friend in San Diego, Calvin, my business adviser for the past 20 years, Robert, my best friend, and Jan, Julie's sister, who threw me the #BestEver birthday party in Rancho Santa Fe, CA. I know what you must be thinking. Did he call in a small nation to weigh in on who would be the next woman in his life? The answer is yes, I did, because I was totally lost. Online dating struck me as an online meat market where the one who has the best features, the best abs, bones, curves and inspired introductions wins the prize.

With the help of my friends, I met some incredible women this way. But if one of them was ready to settle down into a more serious relationship, I would admit that I was still trying to find myself and that I needed more time. More time—more time for what exactly? What does that empty, non-committal statement even mean?

The truth is, I should have listened to Anita.

I SHOULD HAVE WAITED & HEALED.

I admit, I may have unintentionally hurt some of the women I dated. Please forgive me if you are one of those women. It was never premeditated. I was a wounded man looking for love in all the wrong places and searching for tenderness in all the wrong faces. I know now that it takes years of growth, maturity and new levels of self-awareness to see the error of your ways.

⇒REFLECTION⇐

No one told me that different dating apps mean different things. Just because you swipe right and have a match doesn't mean that person is the "one" for you.

> *DON'T BE FOOLED IF YOU START IN ON A TEXTING TANGO AND THINK IT'S GOING SOMEWHERE.*

After a few rounds on the virtual dance floor, the other person will probably "ghost" you. If you, too, are new to the game and totally unfamiliar with this new-age tactic, here is what ghosting means. By technical definition, it's the practice of ending a personal relationship with someone by suddenly, and without explanation, withdrawing from all forms of communication with them.

That's the formal meaning.

Emotionally, it feels like the dating rejection from hell, especially when you are freshly back on the horse. Now, I know when this happens your male ego will question why and wonder if you said or did something wrong.

Let me set you straight:

It's NOT YOU!

Don't worry, the woman you were in contact with didn't get a virtual whiff of your onion breath. But here's the real kicker – the person you've been texting with will have the audacity to "unlike" you and the swipe connect will disappear into a virtual abyss, never to be seen again. But again, don't take it personally. It happens to almost everyone. It happened to me.

RECOMMENDATION

Since every dating app means something different, do your research by asking friends which apps they've used and what they know about each one. Be prepared to hear a variety of opinions, preferences and biases. Sift through their feedback and employ it to help navigate these uncharted waters.

If you decide to post a profile, I strongly suggest you have a female friend do it for you. She will know exactly what will get you a wink, a high five, a smiley face or some other emoji that means you just might be interesting enough. But remember, don't get too excited. You're not in the auditorium yet. You're still driving around the parking lot, eyes peeled on finding an empty space so you don't have to keep circling and circling in hopes of someone noticing you. If you do meet someone but know deep down that you're not ready to settle down or build a relationship or the spark just isn't there, then by all means, don't meet up a second time. It would just be a waste of your time and hers.

You'll know within the first 10 to 15 minutes of meeting someone if this person ignites something within you. Seriously, you'll know. You will hear her voice and something in it will click.

If you meet someone online and you are interested in her, talk to her on the phone for several weeks before you meet face to face. Listen more than you talk and try to hear what she is saying between sentences. Only if you like what you hear over many conversations should you graduate to an in-person meeting.

Finally, I'd recommend not ghosting a woman, even if you have no intention of dating her long-term. Tell her you're not ready. One of my many mistakes with online dating was that I would just disappear without considering how the other person felt. It was wrong.

EMOTIONAL HONESTY

I will start with this thought. Emotional honesty is the combination that opens the vault of a woman's soul.

We've all heard the dreaded question during long car rides or in the quiet of night just before falling asleep: What are you thinking? It's true. Women really want to know what we men are thinking, what we are feeling. And they don't want to have to use the jaws of life to get something out of us.

BUT WE'D RATHER TALK ABOUT ANYTHING ELSE IN THE WORLD THAN OUR FEELINGS, RIGHT?

After all, we were all taught as boys to suck it up, be brave, hide our feelings, act strong, that crying is for the weak. The problem with this is that we men aren't able to be ourselves, maybe we don't even know our real selves. And we sure can't have meaningful relationships with women if we are afraid to uncover our soft underbellies, afraid to let them get to know us because we fear rejection, hurt and embarrassment.

The truth is, fellas, you will never make love or have real intimacy with your wife until you become vulnerable and are able to connect with your inner feelings and express them, until you put your truth on the table, bare, for all to see. There is a dimension to loving your wife that can move beyond intimacy into ecstasy when you two connect emotionally. This only happens when you open up and share your heart. I am 52 as I'm writing this book, and it's taken me 40 years to come to this place of truth.

I am convinced, now more than ever before, that letting go of the need to be affirmed, liked or validated by others is the first step toward being honest with yourself. And men, once you are honest with yourselves, you are free to love yourselves. Until you love yourself, you will never fully love a woman. As I just mentioned in the preceding paragraph, you might have sex, but you'll never make love.

By the way, you'll never keep a woman just because you have sex with her. It may fulfill you, but it will leave her wanting a deeper connection than you're willing or capable of giving.

Emotional honesty doesn't mean you become less masculine or lose your "man card," whatever the heck that is. It's being an MVP (Most Vulnerable Person) and owning it. I believe that when a man becomes truly vulnerable, he doesn't lose anything; rather, he gains everything. He understands that his life is not just about himself.

To become a certified MVP, you have to take off the mask, guys. You have to:

- **Shred the player card.**
- **Delete the little black book.**
- **Overcome the wandering-eye syndrome.**
- **Stop hiding your smartphone (both of them).**
- **Respect all women as if they were your blood sisters.**
- **Have no secrets.**

Emotional honesty means giving the woman you love your cell phone passcode and inviting her to review all of your social media communications. It also means being accountable when you are away from home by sharing your location via your mobile device.

Emotional honesty is admitting that you're sometimes stuck, professionally unfulfilled, immature and still growing in some areas. It's telling her when you feel lost, lonely, confused, discouraged, unhappy or disappointed that you haven't achieved more in life. Better yet, it's sharing with her your hopes, dreams and aspirations.

Instead of receiving your wife or girlfriend's feedback as a personal attack, emotional honesty means being open to what she is saying so you can be a better man, for her, for your family, for the community, for the world and for yourself. Ask her early and often how you can best support her in the endeavors that are important to her.

Gentlemen, please know that having a hard conversation with a woman who "gets you" is sometimes all the therapy you'll ever need in life. A woman can see what you don't see and hear beyond the words that are coming out of your mouth.

In the book *Wild at Heart: Discovering the Secret of a Man's Soul*, author John Eldridge says in the chapter The Father's Voice: "Face your fears head-on.

"DROP THE FIG LEAF: COME OUT FROM HIDING.

For how long?

"Longer than you want to; long enough to raise the deeper issues, let the wound surface from beneath it all."

Until you decide to be totally honest with yourself, you can talk, but your words won't have weight. They'll be empty and hollow because you're speaking from your head instead of your heart.

And hear this, friends:

A WOMAN DOESN'T WANT TO BE TOUCHED BY YOUR HAND UNTIL YOU'VE TOUCHED HER HEART, MIND AND SOUL.

As I said at the beginning of this chapter, once you touch a woman's heart, mind and soul, once you connect with her emotionally, you have the key to unlock and the match to ignite her limitless potential to love.

Paraphrasing Mike Murdock once more: Did you know that a woman wants to be activated rather than tolerated? A man who understands that activating a woman starts with emotional honesty will strike a chord that resonates for generations to come and will unlock the potential within himself, as well as her.

So, the bottom line is simple. A man will unlock his own potential by connecting with a woman who can see through him. The reality is that your woman is already powerful, she is only waiting for you to grasp it and own it so the two of you can catapult one another to new horizons and depths. Now that's a true MVP! I think I hear Salt-N-Pepa singing our theme song: *What a man, what a man, whatta mighty good man!*

⇉RECOMMENDATION⇇

- On a regular basis, Jodi and I check in with each other by asking if the other is getting what he or she needs. Take a moment and ask the woman in your life if her needs are being met. Listen fully. If you are not clear about something, ask her to tell you more. You want to make sure you are really understanding the meaning of what she's saying.

- Ask her what you can do to improve the relationship, your communication and your confidence in what you are building together.

- Share with her what you really think and feel about something that was said publicly or privately.

- Admit it when you make a mistake. Do it quickly.

- Overcommunicate so you are not backpedaling

and having to explain what did or didn't happen, or what is going to happen. Women love details. They don't like being left in the dark or the last ones to find something out. Again, I've learned this one the hard way.

SHARE EARLY AND OFTEN.
IT BUILDS TRUST.

- Be open to revealing that you don't know what you don't know. Chances are good that she knows you don't know. She's just waiting to see if you'll man up and admit it, and if you have the maturity to ask for help.

- If you struggle privately with pornography, gambling, addictions, cheating, stealing, lying, lusting or anything else that will negatively impact your relationship, admit it and then decide to deal with it to overcome it. The great gift of emotional honesty with yourself first and then your spouse is critical to your health, well-being and future.

- Communicate to her if you struggle with being the breadwinner and carrying the financial load for the family. It may be emasculating to admit that, but it will be well worth it in the long run.

[CHAPTER SEVEN]

CORE PHILOSOPHY:

THE ESSENCE OF YOUR SOUL

WHO ARE YOU WHEN NO ONE IS LOOKING?

What have you packed into the metaphorical suitcase you haul around everywhere?

What is driving your car?

What are the principles that serve as the guardrails that keep you on track?

WHO ARE YOU AT YOUR CORE?

What is your core philosophy – the deep values that are central to who you are and who you want to be?

Most importantly, does your behavior reflect those core values?

Do you sometimes, or often, act in ways that contradict your core philosophy? Friends, it's taken me 52 years to get to this point, but I can finally say that I'm now living in alignment with my core values. Instead of livin' the life, I'm now livin' the peace!

How did I do it? By acting like the man I wanted to become instead of the man I was. By living out my core philosophy. Once you start seeing yourself as you want to be, it's like throwing a pebble into a smooth lake. Even a tiny change on the road to living out your core values can ripple farther than you would ever think. Here's the rub, though. Seeing yourself differently isn't a jaunt down easy street. It's hard, it's challenging, it's full of potholes. Just because you are changing and seeing yourself differently, it doesn't mean other people around you will jump onboard right away. The more you depart from what's comfortable for those around you, the more pushback you're likely to receive.

Why do some people attract the wrong people or the wrong opportunities? Because they're re-attracting who they were instead of who they are becoming.

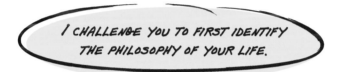

I CHALLENGE YOU TO FIRST IDENTIFY THE PHILOSOPHY OF YOUR LIFE.

And friends, please aim as high as you dare.

This core philosophy should determine what you believe, how you want to behave and how you want to show up in the world. My core philosophy is that I am absolutely brilliant at what I do, and I cut out of my life anyone or any actions that block my brilliance. Does that sound arrogant or haughty? I told you to aim high! (That's the short version. I've included more specific examples later in this chapter.) Anyway, I know that if I don't value me, no one else will.

Next, make sure your core philosophy is ever-evolving. How do you do this? You must constantly apply mental floss to how you are living out your values, how you are bringing everything you have to any given task, to all your close rela- tionships. Get rid of the old thoughts and behaviors that are no longer serving you and that keep you running in place, going nowhere. Don't fall for conformity. Seek to learn, un- learn and re-learn.

As I've said earlier in the book, there was a time in my life when I struggled with low self-esteem. I didn't believe in or have confidence in myself. These feelings of inadequacy caused me to live a very limited life, so much so that I turned down a job I didn't feel worthy of. I was holding myself back. My real core philosophy (even if it was subconscious then) was rooted in who I was instead of who I wanted to become. Often, it's not who you actually are that holds you back from being your most brilliant self — it's who you think you're NOT.

REMEMBER, WHAT YOU THINK, YOU BECOME.

If you think you're not equipped to be successful, you won't be.

A woman wants a man who has a rock-solid core philosophy she can respect. Ask her what her core philosophies are, what her beliefs are about faith, friends, finances, fun and the future. However, before you ask her, please make sure you have a good idea of where you stand. This ensures that you won't be swayed by her feedback and adjust your answers to appeal to her heart. That is disingenuous. Ask me how I know? Ummm... let's see, I read it in a book. Not!

This is what I believe at the core of my being:

 SPIRITUALLY

I believe in God. I believe in prayer. I believe, like songwriter B. Brown wrote, Without God, I could do nothing. I am a Christian. The bottom line is that I love God. Every morning, when I see the sun rise, I see God's handiwork. Every time I take a breath, I thank God. This is who I am at my core. In fact, my father gave me the middle name Theophilus, which means "friend of God" in Greek. Yes, I consider myself a friend of God.

But being a Christian doesn't mean I get it right every time. Have I wronged people? Yes. Have I hurt people? Yes. Have I failed people? Yes. But being a dialed-in Christian in this post-modern era means owning your mistakes and asking for forgiveness.

Every day I wake up now, I look for ways to serve others, and thereby God, through my work. I hope the light of Christ shines through everything I do.

HEALTH AND WELLNESS

I take care of my body so I can take care of my family. After landing in the hospital with a kidney stone, I now realize the importance of drinking lots of water.

Diabetes tends to run in my family. As my 81-year-old mother liked to say: "Sugar runs in our family."

After gaining 20 pounds during the height of the pandemic by binging on carbs and sugar, I was feeling sluggish and not sleeping well. My A1C levels were way above what they should have been. I heeded my doctor's advice and changed my eating habits by making healthier choices, got back into an exercise habit, added meditation to my daily routine and started taking sleep seriously. It's paid off, and I feel great.

FAMILY

After not spending enough time with my children when I was always working, always traveling, I have renewed my pledge to be there for them, to love them and hold them in the forefront of my mind always. As Pat Morley wrote in *Man in the Mirror:*

> *BUILD YOUR LIFE AROUND THOSE WHO WILL BE CRYING AT YOUR FUNERAL.*

As divorced parents, Renee and I are making a concerted effort to co-parent civilly and to respect each other. I decided after we divorced that I would joyfully pay her alimony. Instead of being upset or harboring resentment about paying the annual alimony settlement, I hold my breath, pay it before it's due each month and choose joy.

See, our marriage worked until it didn't; Renee is a good woman and I refuse to tear her down in front of my children or say anything evil or negative about her to her face or behind her back. That's not healthy or psychologically sound. I respect her and am thankful to God that she has given me two amazing gifts in Daniel and Madison. I've taken the brunt of the responsibility for our divorce. As a Christian, I've chosen to take the high road: pay up, keep my word, stay connected to my children and wish her well.

 # CAREER/BUSINESS

Seth Godin says, "Doing what you love is for amateurs, however, loving what you do is for professionals." I love this quote. It says everything I believe about my life's work.

 # FINANCIALLY

After running through 8 million dollars in a twenty-year span, I took the advice of David Bach, author of *The Automatic Millionaire.* He said, "Automate your money. What you don't see, you don't spend."

 # SOCIALLY

I believe all people deserve respect. I believe in the dignity of humankind, of every man, woman and child. I believe that those who have your ear, have your life. I try to surround myself with people who challenge me to be a better man.

EDUCATIONALLY

Eric Hoffer said, "In times of change, the learners will inherit the earth while the unlearned will find themselves beautifully equipped to live in a world that no longer exists." I try to learn something new every day. I hope I never stop learning.

 ## EMOTIONALLY

As I have told you in this book, I sat in front of a therapist for 18 months figuring out what I was hiding from, what I was running from, and how my behavior contributed to my unease, my problems and my failed relationships. I'm a new man now, and I'm trying life out as an MVP (Most Valuable Person). So far, so good!

RECOMMENDATION

Ask yourself:

- **Do I commit verbal judo on myself?** Sometimes people beat themselves up by saying things like, "I'm so stupid. I'm so dumb. Why do I keep doing this? I'll never succeed." If this is part of your core philosophy, you are most likely engaging in self-sabotaging actions and behaviors. You need to learn to reframe your self-defeating state of mind to craft a positive core philosophy.

- **Do I continue to go in circles in relationships, in beliefs, in outcomes?** Why do I always end up at the same place? If yes is your answer, then your core philosophy likely focuses on who you are instead of who you want to become. Ask yourself who you want to become and how you can construct a core philosophy that will get you there.

- **Why me? Why now?** Yes, it's, time to step up and own where you want to go, who you want to become, what you want to do and who you want to be with.

After thinking through these questions, try writing out your core philosophy. Keep it short so you will remember it when you are faced with choices and decisions. Write a sentence, a phrase or create a bucket list if you want. If you get stuck, check out this source: *7 Tips for Developing Your Personal Philosophy,* written by Jim Rohn (Success.com, Aug 9, 2015).

- Set your sail – examine what you do and how you think during life's shifts.

- Learn from your successes and your failures, as well as those of others.

- Read all you can.

- Keep a journal.

- Observe and listen.

- Be disciplined.

- Don't neglect to take care of the important things in your life.

- Do good.

Once you have a good sense of your personal philosophy, put it to the test. Remind yourself of it throughout your day as you make decisions and talk to members of the opposite sex. Run your thoughts, actions and behaviors through your philosophy filter, and let it guide you.

If your core philosophy states that you are ever growing and learning and your boss approaches you with a new project, you'll look at it as an opportunity to learn and grow instead of just another task. If your core philosophy states that you are happy, whole and capable, you'll pass on relationships that make you feel less than who you know you are, knowing you are capable of taking care of yourself until you find the friendship or partner who speaks to the music in your soul. If your core philosophy states that you embrace change and can easily adjust to life's shifts, then you won't run for cover or comfort when you face a major transition in life. Instead, you'll tackle it head on with enthusiasm.

As I've alluded to in this chapter, your personal philosophy guides your character. Character is defined by the American Heritage Dictionary of the English Language as "the combination of qualities or features that distinguishes one person, group or thing from another... the combined moral or ethical structure of a person or group."

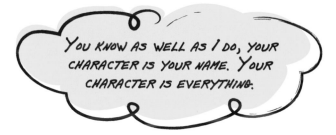

> YOU KNOW AS WELL AS I DO, YOUR CHARACTER IS YOUR NAME. YOUR CHARACTER IS EVERYTHING.

During the pandemic, I visited one of my mentors, Wintley Phipps, a world-renowned vocal artist, education activist, pastor and CEO/founder of U.S. Dream Academy. He's had the honor of performing for six U.S. presidents, appeared on Oprah's OWN and been married to his wife, Linda, for 42 years.

I asked my friend what the key to thriving in life is, and without batting an eye, he answered with one word:

CHARACTER.

He went on to say that men needed to be especially careful with romances and finances. He said that any man of substantial character does not chase girls, gold or glory. They are the ones who take care not to be overexposed and underdeveloped. "Sometimes you can have talent that will take you to the top," he said, "but only your character will keep you there."

Many years ago, I was in Singapore having dinner when a young lady in the restaurant caught my eye, and we struck up a conversation. The next thing I knew, we were at a nightclub where there was another brother she knew. The three of us were talking, having fun, and the drinks were flowing. Now, anyone who knows me knows that I don't drink. (It's another one of my core values.) But here I was, halfway around the world and who was going to know if I had a sip or two? Did I mention I was married and had two young children at home?

Well, as the evening progressed, something seemed off to me. The other brother said we should go party somewhere else, and our female companion was all for it. She said, "C'mon, Simon, you'll enjoy it." My spider sense (defined as an extraordinary ability to sense imminent danger) started tingling and I knew I had to get out of this situation quickly. I excused myself to the restroom, which was conveniently, and mercifully, located next to the entrance/exit. After leaving the men's room, I headed out the front door fast. I felt the 3 a.m. summer humidity slap me in the face as if to say, "What were you thinking?" I hailed a taxi, got to my hotel room and locked the door behind me. I had the sense that I'd just dodged a bullet, maybe literally. Anything could have happened that night, and probably most of it not good. My character had been called into question, and I had almost lost it.

My mentor, Dr. Mark Chironna, has often said that the road to true character is narrow and follows a straight line in one direction. In other words, a man with character doesn't get easily sidetracked by distractions of convenience, comfort or coolness. A person of character will walk alone in order to protect his or her name instead of feeling the need to join the crowd.

Let me tell it to you straight. Character is music to a woman's soul. A woman wants a man whose character doesn't waffle, whose head doesn't turn with the wind (or toward another female, I should add), whose actions and words match and are always respectful, kind and loving. A woman wants a man who has moral integrity, a love of learning, patience and self-control. There's a proverb that says a man with self-control is stronger than a warrior who can take a city.

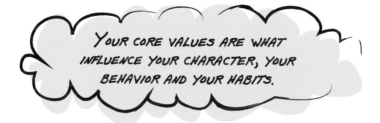

YOUR CORE VALUES ARE WHAT INFLUENCE YOUR CHARACTER, YOUR BEHAVIOR AND YOUR HABITS.

Keep them front and center all the time, my friends.

REFLECTION

What percolates in your mind as you think about your personal character?

What guides you?

⇉RECOMMENDATION⇇

- Surround yourself with a small group of guys who cherish their wives and love raising their children. Yes, it's true, iron sharpens iron.

- If you are single, find at least one male friend who challenges you to be a better man. If you're hanging out with people who run women down, disrespect them, enjoy their wandering eyes or chase skirts, as they say, then drop them immediately. You'll be much better off without them!

[CHAPTER EIGHT]

GET TO THE
POINT

Here's what I know to be true after 50-plus years on this earth and 30-plus years of observing women.

By the way, this is my reflection and recommendation all rolled into one.

- **Never believe that the right person will come along.** Believe you are the right person, and, in time, you will select someone you want to share your life with.

- **Come into a relationship whole.** Anyone who tells you that you complete them is not the one. Run, don't walk, the other way. A couple should be like a puzzle with two pieces. Each piece is intact, and when put together they make a nicer picture.

- **How a person does small things is how they do everything.** It took me 10 years to really get the power of this statement. If you want to know what someone is really like, take them to a restaurant and observe how they treat the wait staff. It will tell you everything you need to know about their values, their core philosophies.

Men are simple. Feed us, love us, respect us.

- **Women are complex.** A woman wants you to talk to her. Okay, that's not an earth-shattering revelation. But please open your mouth and have something meaningful to say. I'm not asking you to quote Plato, Socrates, Tupac or Cornel West. But for goodness' sake, please don't fill the space with hot air or a ton of random statements and word fillers. These are cop-outs. Ask me how I know. I've been there,

I've said those things. Get real and get honest with yourself and with her. Tell her what's in your heart instead of what you think she wants to hear. If you've reached the next level of emotional availability and intelligence, then take the leap toward reading her body language, recalling what she has said over and over and listening to what is not being said in order to tap into her mental, spiritual and emotional frame of mind.

- **Cherishing a woman goes far deeper than loving a woman.** Anyone can say, "I love you." However, when you cherish a woman, you will die for her. If you can't cherish her, don't waste her time.

- **A man is never in charge of the home.** Go ahead and accept this truth now.

A WOMAN MAY LET HER MAN THINK HE IS IN CHARGE, BUT DON'T BE FOOLED; IT'S ALWAYS HER.

- **Pre-marital counseling is highly recommended.** These are the things you'll discover in pre-marital counseling: What are your deep core values? What sets you off? What gets on your nerves? How do you want to parent together if you decide to have children or are raising children from a previous marriage? What is your faith or relationship with God? How did you form your values, what are they and how do they align with your fiancé's values? Is there anything in your history that needs to be processed? Pre-marital counseling pulls back the covers and reveals what each of you thinks about communication, money and sex. This is where you get everything out on the table, where you reaffirm compatibility.

- **In a relationship, be the best person you can be.** No one is perfect and no one is perfect for you. Ask questions. Listen to her responses. Expose her to your family and friends early and often. See if you strike a chord with her family and friends and if the same happens to her.

- **Ask this question:**

IF I WERE TO TALK TO YOUR FORMER SPOUSE OR BOYFRIEND ABOUT WHY YOU GOT DIVORCED OR BROKE UP, WHAT WOULD HE SAY?

- **Furthermore, ask her about her relationship with the other male figures in her life, especially her father.**

- **Keep your eyes open and your ears in tune.** There are three truths – yours, hers and somewhere in the middle is the real truth. Remember that you don't usually see things as they are, you see them as you are.

- **Beware of people who are married or open to marriage but are not marriage minded.** Married men need to be careful about being friends with other women. And vice-versa. Married women need to be careful about being friends with other men. If you have a female friend, by all means, introduce her to your spouse, then let your spouse decide if this friendship can continue or needs to end.

THAT'S RIGHT, YOUR WIFE SHOULD HAVE THE FINAL SAY.

- I'll give you an example from my own life. Because of the business I'm in, I have had a few close, platonic female friendships. With Jodi in the picture, that became a problem. She wanted to be the only woman I ever needed to talk to, and I got it. I wanted to be the only man she needed to talk to as well. This meant that we both had to cut our ties with friends or past relationships with the opposite sex. We were choosing to find a third door together and close any previous doors that could impact our impending marriage. We didn't want to compete for each other's hearts. We each wanted to be Number One to each other. We also made a commitment to find married-couple friends to spend quality time with.

- **Don't waste her time.** As I said before, you'll know within the first 10 or 15 minutes of meeting a woman whether this relationship has a future.

- **If you're not going to marry her, it's best not to sleep with her.** Have enough respect for her and for yourself not to open that door.

- **Divorce is death by a thousand cuts.** Every day, decide to be better instead of bitter. Dr. Edwin Louis Cole used to say, "There are only two things you do in life. You enter and you exit." How you exit a relationship determines how you will enter the next one.

- **Every man needs a therapist.** As I said earlier, the last thing I wanted to do was sit on a sofa and spill my guts to a woman named Anita. Guess what, though? If it weren't for the prayers of the folks at my church, Phyllis Day and Aunt Rosa (my second mom), along with Anita, I don't think I would have made it. It was those people who helped me reclaim custody of myself. They provided my breakthrough.

LOVE
WITH NO STRINGS
ATTACHED

Valentine's Day comes without fail every single year – that dreaded annual commercial celebration of romantic love. So many of us men find ourselves scrambling to come up with the perfect, last-minute card, box of chocolates, bouquet of flowers or perhaps a nice piece of jewelry on this contrived day of love.

But fabricated as the February 14th occasion is, it seems to work its magic, nonetheless. In 2020, when Valentine's Day spending reached its height, Americans shelled out about $28 billion on date night activities and gifts, with men spending twice as much as women, according to the National Retail Federation.

It's not just about the bottom line, though.

COUPLES MAKE PLANS OR SURPRISE ONE ANOTHER ON VALENTINE'S DAY.

They go out to dinner and talk to each other about why they fell in love. They remember. They forgive and forget. They hold hands, they touch.

THEY MAKE AN EFFORT.

True story: A man named Joseph Andrew Dekenipp escaped an Arizona jail in 2014 by crawling over razor wire and climbing two fences in order to spend Valentine's Day with his girlfriend, as reported by CNN affiliate KTVK. He was later captured in a bar about 10 miles from the detention center. Now that's inmate intimate for you!

So, woe to the man in a relationship who forgets to honor Valentine's Day! It's kind of like a Super Bowl for women: They often get just what they need that day – appreciation, thoughtfulness, romance, special treatment.

So, why do we celebrate love just once a year?

Why do we think it's enough to formally connect with each other one day out of 365?

Many years ago, I heard Dr. Edwin Louis Cole, a revered thought leader, speak, and I'll never forget what he said, "Love desires to give at the expense of self."

Back then, 30 years ago, I didn't fully understand what he meant. I was young, self-absorbed and emotionally clueless. Now, I realize that when I choose to love other human beings, it's not about what I can get from them but what I can give to them.

LOVE ISN'T LOVE
UNTIL YOU GIVE IT AWAY.

Love doesn't scream and shout but walks quietly and confidently into the room. It identifies a need and solves it without fanfare.

Love doesn't seek a pat on the back, a plaque to hang on the wall or a press release telling the world how great it is.

Love doesn't distinguish by skin color, socioeconomic status or education level.

I can't say it any better than apostle Paul did in his letter to the Corinthians.

Here's Corinthians 13, verses 4-8:

Love is patient, love is kind. It does not envy, it does not boast, it is not proud. It does not dishonor others, it is not self-seeking, it is not easily angered, it keeps no record of wrongs. Love does not delight in evil but rejoices with the truth. It always protects, always trusts, always hopes, always perseveres.

Okay, time to stop talking about love and start doing love right.

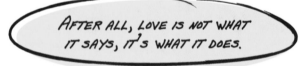

AFTER ALL, LOVE IS NOT WHAT IT SAYS, IT'S WHAT IT DOES.

Love is not a passing thought. It's making those you say you love a priority, and it's doing what you say you're going to do. Love supersedes hate. It can overcome the barriers of disagreement. We live in such a divisive, polarized world right now. Let us bring love to the table.

RECOMMENDATION

REACH OUT.

Look through your phone contacts and social media accounts and find those people with whom you have a rapport but maybe haven't spoken to in a while. Contact them. This doesn't have to be hard – it can be a text, a video, a call, an email or even a handwritten note.

Just say, "I'm thinking of you, or I just want you to know I appreciate you and everything you've done for me." Do this on a daily or a weekly basis. No need to wait for Valentine's Day.

What if this simple act spurred others to do the same? Think about the positive chain of events you could set into motion by showing a little love.

PAY ATTENTION.

I recently found myself in a great vintage bookstore while on a business trip. I immediately thought of my daughter, an avid reader with an old soul (as well as a 4.25 GPA – proud papa here!).

She'd asked me to look for a copy of *The Great Gatsby,* and lo and behold, there it was. She'd asked me for a few other titles, too, namely *The Pelican Brief* and *The Notebook.* I was able to snag those also, and I'm planning to give them to her as a surprise.

Knowing my daughter's love of reading, I took that moment in the bookstore to cherish the thought of her and do something special for her to show my love. The act was truly sparking the power of one of the most exceptional and beloved women in my life.

In order to take intentional action, look around to see how you can help with a kind, encouraging word. This small step can go a long way. We can always find an opportunity to uplift someone else.

 ## LOVE THOSE WHO CAN DO NOTHING FOR YOU.

During the last government shutdown and the COVID-19 pandemic, I was really impacted by the number of organizations that stepped forward to aid those who weren't receiving paychecks. For me, these acts of kindness by corporations to lighten the load for those suffering highlighted what we're made of as Americans. Though our history is oppressive and tragic, we, as a whole, are a caring and compassionate nation.

Yes, we can all do something – whether it's providing a meal or donating to a food bank. I invite you to look around within your own community and find a need you can serve.

**I brought up sex and intimacy earlier in the book,
but let's take the subject a bit further.**

Sex – the outward manifestation of love, the very act of love, the only deed that has the power to create life and destroy it.

We all know it, but I'm still going to say it. A man wants sex. A man needs sex.

And a man hopes that his wife wants him as much as he wants her, without him having to beg and plead.

I have a female friend who recently told me this: *If my husband wants to enter the church on Sunday, he needs to have worshiped all week long!*

Get it?

WE MEN NEED TO PAY ATTENTION TO THE DETAILS THAT MAKE OUR WIVES OR GIRLFRIENDS HAPPY.

We need to treat them with honor, respect, appreciation and love all week long. And it's not just because we want sex with her, it's so the sex can please her as much as it pleases us. It's so we can ignite her and thereby light our own flames.

The journey to igniting the power of the woman in your life doesn't just happen by accident. It's a daily choice. It's an emotional commitment that says, I want to be here, instead of an emotionless commitment that says, *I have to be here. I have bills to pay, babies to feed.*

HERE ARE SOME PRACTICAL TIPS TO SPARK ⚡ A WOMAN'S ROMANTIC LOVE.

I'm sharing them with you because I've dropped the ball in so many of these areas so many times, and I'm hoping you don't make the same mistakes I did.

- **Kiss her on the forehead before you leave her presence.**

- **Tell her often how you are a better man because of her.**

- **Send her flowers for no reason.**

- **Leave her love notes.**

- **Cook dinner for her.** If that's way out of your comfort zone, buy a prepared meal. She'll appreciate the gesture.

- **Take the trash out and replace the garbage bag.**

- **Put the toilet seat down.**

- **Make the bed in the morning.**

- **Make her a cup of coffee and bring it to her if she's still in bed.**

- **Iron your own shirts.**

- **Walk the dog.**

- **Do the dishes.**

- **Put the clothes in the washing machine and then the dryer** (that is, if she trusts you and has shown you how to do the laundry correctly).

- **Open the door for her and pull out her chair before she sits down.** (Be sure to push it back in when she does take her seat!)

- **If you're at a restaurant, stand if she gets up to leave the room.**

- **Put gas in her car and wash it.**

- **Show ambition and communicate your plans.**

- **Be realistic.** She'll have no problem sharing your dreams as long as they are grounded with good sense and a plan of action.

- **Listen to her feedback, to her intuition about people, problems and processes.**

- **Make sure you communicate love with the tone of your voice.**

- **Constantly think of ways to show her you love her for no reason.**

- **Make sure she feels secure in her relationship with you.** When a woman feels assured in a relationship, it unlocks the deep well of her soul and causes her to love in ways even she didn't fathom were possible.

- **Be interested.** When she is talking, put your phone down and look her in the eyes like she is the most important person in the world.

- **Talk to her throughout the day, via text, email or by phone.**

- **Write her a letter.** I know it's old-fashioned, but do it anyway. If that's too hard, write on a three-by-five index card. "I cherish you. I need you. I want you. I don't want to do life without you."

- **Meditate with her, read the same book or poem, workout together.**

- **Make it your mission to serve her.**

I can hear some of you guys now saying, "But, Simon, a lot of those actions are women's work." Hear me loud and clear, fellas: That era passed a while ago. So, get with it. Maybe you'll like the way you look in an apron. For sure, she will!

REFLECTION

According to a 2020 article by Morgan Greenwood in *Best Life* magazine, people in loving relationships lead far healthier lives than those who are not. Happily married people experience less stress, heal from health issues faster and live longer than single, divorced or unhappily married people, the article states. Well, that's pretty much common sense, right?

But did you know that cuddling with your spouse or girlfriend releases powerful happy hormones? That staring into each other's eyes for three minutes leads both of your hearts to beat in sync? That love triggers the same response in our brains as painkillers? These facts I read in the same article.

Of course love matters, but it's more important than you can imagine to have good love. That takes work. It takes dedication. It takes communication. C'mon, guys, it's more than worth it.

Your very life depends on it!

[CHAPTER TEN]

THE
MUSIC
OF HER
SOUL

In Buffalo, NY, where I grew up, we used to go to late-night gospel concerts at church. I remember hearing incredible musicians who had learned to play by ear.

You might be wondering what that phrase "play by ear" means. In *Popular Music* (1996): *Volume 15-Issue 2* published by Cambridge University Press, Lars Lilliestam says, "The vast majority of all music ever made is played by ear. To make music by ear means to create, perform, remember and teach music without the use of written notation. This is a type of music-making that has been little observed by musicology, which has mainly been devoted to notated music."

The musicians we listened to at our church would stand back and listen to what the performer was doing, then jump in and make it a full-on party of instruments and voices. I specifically remember the organist, a man named Eric Reed, who would play without knowing the notes beforehand, behind the singer, who was belting out lyrics from the depths of his soul. It was as if they had been performing together for years. It was nothing short of a miraculous spiritual experience that always left me wanting more.

I started thinking about it.

EVERY ONE OF US MEN HAS THE OPPORTUNITY AND THE ABILITY TO LEARN TO PLAY BY EAR WITH THE WOMEN WE LOVE.

What do I mean by that?

I mean we can bend into the rhythms she's creating from her heart and soul. We can listen to the vibrations coming from deep inside her and then join in to make her song more powerful, more symphonic, more complex.

Let's take the metaphor further, shall we?

A relationship that relies on written notation – memorized, rehearsed and routine notes – is mechanical, stale, the same old same old. It's you playing chopsticks while she's longing for Beethoven's *Fifth,* Handel's *Messiah* or Mozart's *Requiem.* We can't be satisfied with pounding on the xylophone while she's got the skills to play several instruments at once.

Men, we have to learn to stay in tune with the women we love. If we want to ignite the power and potential in them, we must hear the music in their souls – the haunting trill of a lonely oboe, the bold crescendo of a pair of cymbals, the sweet chords of a melodic piano, the intense booming of the thundering bass drum and the soft highs of a whole section of violins. And then, we need to join her in song, creating harmony, counterpoint and fusion.

Don't worry. I'm not asking you to drop what you're doing and apply to Juilliard.

I'M SIMPLY ASKING YOU NOT TO BE TONE-DEAF.

To listen to her, observe her moods, her highs, her lows. Join in her happiness, her sadness, her fears and struggles, her hopes and dreams. Jump right in. Become the lyrics to her song, the beat to her score, the rhythm to her blues, the rock to her roll, the country to her western.

How, you ask?

⇒RECOMMENDATION⇐

Study your woman like you research investing in stocks or buying crypto, like you follow your favorite sports teams, like you keep up with the latest trends in music, cars or whatever you're into. It'll take work, but it's work you've got to do.

A fact sheet for Haze Guitars states, "Your guitar may sound out of tune on certain chords, or in certain positions on the neck, while it sounds okay in other places. The important thing is that the tuning remains stable in the position where you originally tuned."

I know that sounds confusing, but here's the gist. If you're out of tune with your wife or girlfriend, go back to the beginning, to when you first fell in love. Remember the nonstop texting, the constant communication, the way your heart beat faster whenever you saw her, how she took your breath away and how you went around town with the biggest smile on your face? It's not gone, that excitement, that romantic love, it's just buried under life's burdens.

Here are some ideas for staying in tune with your woman. Practice them like Mrs. Teas (my friend's exacting piano teacher) made her students practice their scales, over and over and over, ad nauseam.

- **Know her favorites.** What's her favorite color? What's her favorite restaurant, song, flower, saying, quote, book, poem? Once you know, use that golden information. Take her to that restaurant, buy her those flowers, have that song playing when she gets home, read that book, recite that poem. Buy her a piece of clothing that's her favorite color.

- **We've always heard that the way to a man's heart is through his stomach. Well, I believe the same is true of a woman.** Find out what her favorite foods are and cook them for her. If she's into Italian, make some wonderful kind of pasta. If she's into health food, make it vegetarian or vegan. Google recipes. Or, if your budget can afford, hire a personal chef.

WARNING, ASK HER FIRST BEFORE YOU START MESSING AROUND IN HER KITCHEN.

- **Consistently surprise her.** Keep her on her toes and waiting expectantly to see what you'll do next.

- **It's common at weddings and couples' retreats to hear that a strand of three chords is not easily broken.** The reference is that God is the third chord that holds the marriage together. Was your marriage or relationship made in heaven? Do you truly believe it was meant to be? Ordained on high? If so, doesn't that make you want to work hard and harder to make it sacred?

Have you ever watched the movie *The Notebook* based on the book written by Nicholas Sparks? I highly recommend it. Years ago, Super Bowl champion and megawatt television host Michael Strahan commented, "*The Notebook* gets me every time. It's a great love story. Girl from a wealthy family, boy from the wrong side of the tracks. They get on each other's nerves, but they can't live without each other. They were absolutely meant to be together. That's the kind of love I'm talking about."

- **Release the need to control.** I'm talking about life, situations, other people and, certainly, your wife or girlfriend. Compliment her rather than nag about what is wrong with her.

- **Grow with her.** A wife doesn't need the same things from you after you've had children together that she did before. She'll need a whole lot more of you! She needs more from you if she's going through hard times than when life seems easy to her. Be there for her.

REFLECTION

So, what happens when the music stops?

Using the old American children's game of musical chairs as an analogy, the music has suddenly stopped and a seat has also been removed.

Listen, I didn't get divorced because I was running into the arms of another woman. I got divorced because we lost the rhythm of love. We were off-key, out of tune and our timing wasn't in sync.

We just weren't able to hit the right chords with each other anymore.

Instead of hitting middle "C " for cherish, compliment and compatibility, I was striking a "G" for goodness' sake, I don't want to be here anymore.

I don't wish divorce on anyone. But sometimes it's the right, the honest, thing to do.

If you both want to work it out together, there still and always will be a way to blend your particular notes and sounds so you can play harmoniously again. I've said it once or twice, but I'll say it again. If you're in big trouble as a couple, it's a good idea to get professional help, whether it's from a pastor at your church or a licensed family therapist.

Remember, every single note has a sound that stirs a vibration that lasts long after the music has stopped.

A NOTE IS A WORD.
USE YOUR WORDS CAREFULLY IN THE COMPANY OF WOMEN.

Let your words sing.

Let them bring forth the music in the souls of the women around you.

[CHAPTER ELEVEN]

JODI
AND ME

I will never forget the night I met my current wife, Jodi. Yes, after several false starts, I eventually healed and regrouped enough to jump back into the dating scene. We officially met on a dating website.

Okay, don't shoot me. I know, I know. I had previously vowed never, ever to participate in online dating again.

That was after a handful of weird experiences and me discovering that I wasn't ready to date after all. But I thought Jodi was different. After meeting virtually, she and I began talking nonstop via texts, emails and phone calls.

And then in blew Hurricane Dorian, the Category 5 monster that devastated areas of the Bahamas in early September 2019. Weather forecasters were predicting the storm would head on over to Florida and strongly encouraged residents to evacuate. We attempted to book flights out, but the Orlando airport was closed. I decided to take my family to the Waldorf Astoria right in the heart of Walt Disney World and ride the hurricane out there. If we were going to lose our home, at least we would be safe at the happiest place on earth.

I had so enjoyed my fluid, easy talks with Jodi, and I didn't want to hit the pause button on our blooming relationship. At the Waldorf, I remember waking up in the middle of the night to send her texts. Early mornings I spent locked in the bathroom chatting with her on my phone. I know my son was wondering what the heck was up with me.

THERE WAS SOMETHING SPECIAL ABOUT THIS WOMAN, AND THE CURIOUS GEORGE IN ME HAD TO FIND OUT.

After almost 36 hours of back-and-forth communication with Jodi, I decided it was time to meet her.

Tired of room service, my children asked for takeout one night, so I suggested grabbing chicken wings from a popular wing joint. I sent Jodi a text that said, "Would you like to come over here and meet me in the parking lot, if only for a few minutes?"

She said "yes," that she could be there in 30 or 45 minutes, and suddenly I got nervous. Excited, sure, but also nervous. In one of his comedy routines, Chris Rock jokes that when you meet someone for the first time, you aren't really meeting them, you're meeting their representative.

Anyway, this was as far from the truth as it could have been when I met Jodi.

When I saw her, I gave her a hug and I didn't want to ever let go. We huddled in my car like two high school sweethearts, making googly eyes at each other. I could hear Percy Sledge singing in my ear, *When a man loves a woman, can't keep his mind on nothin' else.*

There she was in the flesh. She did exist. She was real!

We talked, we laughed, we hugged, we smooched.

After hugging goodbye, we promised we'd call each other. I made sure she was safely in her car and told her to text me when she got home. Why do men do this? I have no idea. Common sense says that they'd for sure call if there was something wrong. I guess it's natural – part of our protective natures. And perhaps it's an unconscious way to store up brownie points in the relationship bank account. I don't know if that's true, it's just my two cents' worth.

Fast forward.

Obviously, we survived Dorian and being in close quarters away from home. We checked out of the hotel and I dropped the family off, practically speeding away because I couldn't wait to talk more freely with Jodi. My feelings had been stirred and were roiling at this point.

I FELT LIKE I WAS 14 AND
IN LOVE.

I called Jodi that day and we made plans to connect for an official date later on. I told her I had a special surprise for our first date, and she agreed to come. Now, mind you, she didn't really know me. She hadn't had time to run a background check on me, find out my credit score, verify if I was gainfully employed or searching for a sugar mama. Though we'd talked at length, she didn't know if I was a Republican, a Democrat or an Independent. She trusted me despite all that. Of course she had everyone important in her life tracking our every move, I found out later.

I picked her up and, as we were driving down the road, I turned to Jodi and said, "I'm taking you to Tuesday night Bible study at my church." She looked at me like, okay, that's different, but went right along with it. I had decided that if she was the one for me, our spiritual values had to align and there was no time like the present to find out. She enjoyed the service and the discussion. I took her home and we talked for hours on the phone the next day.

Fast forward.

Forty-five days into our new relationship, I had to go on a business trip.

THINGS WERE GOING SO WELL BETWEEN US, BUT I STARTED TO SECOND-GUESS MYSELF.

Was this too good to be true? Were we moving too fast? Admittedly, I was still smarting from my divorce, also. Once I got to San Diego, I decided that I needed to hit the brakes.

I called Jodi and broke up with her that same day.

Why didn't I do the manly thing and talk to her face-to-face? Why did I not just talk to her about my feelings instead of taking the coward's way out?

Well, sometimes you can lead a horse to water, but you can't make him drink.

**I was acting like my old self, the person
I was before therapy.**

THE MAN WHO RAN. THE MAN WHO NEEDED TO ALWAYS BE IN CONTROL.

After we broke up, we both tried dating other people, but none of those relationships went anywhere or lasted very long. I continued to call Jodi, text her off and on, and she continued to respond.

I missed her. So, one night during the height of the pandemic, I called Jodi and told her we needed to talk. I wanted to be with her and had since we had first met, but to tell you the truth, I was scared. I had made so many mistakes before in my relationships. I didn't want to fail again. I had jumped headfirst into relationships too quickly in the past. That was my track record, and I didn't want to repeat it with Jodi.

I knew I still needed more time to work on myself, more time spent in therapy. I just wasn't ready to lock it down with her forever. You can say I had commitment issues for sure. I think I also struggled with her race. Jodi doesn't look like my mother. I have stood and publicly avowed in front of thousands of people that love and respect have no color. But I worried about what people would say. I had pretty much kept my relationship with Jodi a secret.

So, what happened to make me change my mind?

I just knew I couldn't let her get away.

SHE WAS THE REAL DEAL, THE ONE IN A MILLION.

Jodi is one of the kindest people you'll ever meet. She never misses a chance to help someone in need, and she had calmly and compassionately helped me out of my funk.

She's also one of the toughest people I've ever met. She'll fight and fight hard for the people she loves and for the causes she holds dear.

And the cherry on top... she instantly bonded with my mother. Now, they're actually on the phone every day for an hour or more.

As I'm writing this book, Jodi and I have been married for over a year. Yes, we're still kind of newlyweds, but we've also taken off the rose-colored glasses and decided to live intentionally, in close communication and as strong support systems for each other.

Blending two families has not been easy. We've had our bumps. Jodi is a big holiday person and loves giving gifts. I am the polar opposite. I'm not what I'd call a Scrooge; I am kind and I do give presents but, frankly, I prefer to watch football and basketball on television or *Jason Bourne* re-runs, *Shawshank Redemption*, the first *Coming to America* or anything with Denzel Washington, Wesley Snipes, Samuel L. Jackson, Gene Hackman or Anthony Hopkins.

Jodi likes big family gatherings. Holidays haven't been my favorite thing for the past seven years because I knew Renee and I were falling apart as a family unit. Holidays were sad for me. Add to that the true fact that at my core, I'm a loner. As strange as it may sound to you, I'm a socialized introvert. Slowly and surely, though, Jodi has cracked my ultra-private shell and helped me open up.

We are still a work in progress, Jodi and me.

WE'RE LEARNING HOW TO EFFECTIVELY COMMUNICATE AS A BLENDED FAMILY.

I decided I wasn't going to force a relationship with Jodi's daughters, Ashley and Chelsey. I know they are smart young ladies, and they check the temperature of our relationship based on the vibes they get from Jodi. They know I'm avail-able if they need me. We intentionally bring all four children together to celebrate special occasions. They have grown to love each other.

Jodi is my wife and my best friend. We are not perfect. We are just trying to figure out our lives together, model peace and harmony, and love each other. We've intentionally chosen to grow in love after having fallen in love. For us, love is not just an emotion, it's a choice we make every single day.

⇉REFLECTION⇇

A friend of mine, Bob Harrison, once said, "If you meet a woman who has 80 percent of what you need, then you can figure out the other 20 percent together." Jodi and I have committed to communicating and figuring things out. We've had our moments of heated discussions and have found a way to work through whatever is going on. We text each other throughout the day and check in at a minimum if we are not in the same location.

I truly believe I am a better man because I'm married to Jodi. I cherish her as a human being. Instead of shrinking, thinking small and struggling with low self-esteem, I'm able to believe in myself again because of her. In my previous marriage, I was a human ATM machine, funding a rich lifestyle. Don't get me wrong, I still like nice things. But we'd gotten carried away with it. Our possessions were possessing us.

Jodi has helped me understand how to communicate better, with her and with other people.

How have I ignited Jodi's particular power?

When we first started dating, Jodi told me she enjoyed painting. I was thinking that she liked to paint by numbers to relax, but then I saw one of her works. Friends, I'm not exaggerating when I tell you that she's a female Picasso! Well, when we got married, Jodi had stopped painting for several years. I encouraged her to pick it back up. She did just that and, lo and behold, my baby was asked to submit a piece to a prestigious art museum in Philadelphia. She's also entered her work in an art competition, which she had never done before.

So, hopefully we can keep on supporting each other, encouraging each other and igniting the fires inside of each other. I've promised to make that a priority every single day. And, I'll tell you straight, it's a helluva way to live!

RECOMMENDATION

As for practical tips to spark a woman's brilliance and love, here are a few things I know to be true from my first year of being married to Jodi:

- **Honor her when you are with her and when you're away from her.**

- **Pray with her.**

- **Read the word of God together.**

- **Ask her often about her hopes and dreams. Share your own with her.**

- **Write her notes and display them prominently throughout the house.**

- **Text her and touch base with her during the day.**

- **Surprise her and take her out to dinner.** On the other hand, you may want to give her a heads-up. Women like to be dressed appropriately for the setting they are entering.

- **Love her children.**

- **Plan well in advance how you will celebrate her birthday, anniversary or other special occasion.** Show her that she is a priority.

- **It's fine to buy cards for special occasions, but make sure you express yourself in your own words, too.**

- **Work hard to secure her future.**

- **In social situations, keep your eyes and attention focused on her, never on another woman.**

- **Learn her love language and make sure you meet her needs.**

MEN, IT DOESN'T TAKE A LOT OF MONEY TO SHOWER YOUR WIFE OR SIGNIFICANT OTHER WITH ADORATION & ATTENTION.

I heard a story once about a woman who would make her husband's lunch every morning and send him off to work with it. One morning, she woke up hungrier than normal and couldn't resist taking a bite out of the sandwich she'd made him. She worried all day that maybe he'd be irked about that. But he came home and told her that because she'd taken that bite, he'd thought of her all afternoon and couldn't wait to get home to see her. Well, she was nobody's fool. From that day on, she sunk her teeth into his sandwich every single day.

IGNITE THE POWER OF WOMEN IN BUSINESS

As a businessman, I owe a great deal of my success to women. Three female executives, in particular, have helped shape and inspire me to become the person I am today. I owe them much more than thanks and am grateful to call them my mentors.

Pat Engfer, for whom I worked at Hyatt Hotels and Resorts in Florida, taught me how to listen intuitively, how to assess what is really being said at that specific moment, and then how to respond with clarity and insight instead of with emotion. I used to speak from my ego and from my need to appear great, but I learned from Pat how to speak from my heart and add substance to a conversation by listening more intently.

Valerie Ferguson, Director of Lodging for Walt Disney Parks and Resorts, polished me. It was she who taught me about executive presence, how to look and act the part, how to articulate with power and passion and how to use my intelligence most effectively. Valerie, the first African American female to preside over the American Hotel and Motel Association, is the one who told me never to forget where I came from.

THROUGH WORDS AND ACTIONS, SHE TAUGHT ME THE IMPORTANCE OF GIVING BACK.

No longer am I satisfied with just giving a "hand out" to others. Now, I try to give them a "hand up" as well.

Jan Bateman, a marketing executive in tourism, launched me in my sales career. Jan always believed in me, gave me room to make mistakes and allowed me to learn from them. Instead of spoon-feeding me the answers, she made sure I did things on my own. She let me negotiate with clients the way I thought best. I made some costly blunders, of course, but I learned many more priceless lessons.

From all three of these exceptional women, I learned the immense value of what is uniquely female and the importance of applying those traits in Corporate America.

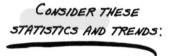

CONSIDER THESE STATISTICS AND TRENDS:

- **Women represent $7 trillion in consumer spending.**

- **Women make 85% of all consumer purchases; 90% of all vacation plans; 75% of all healthcare decisions; and 62% of all car purchases.**

ADD TO THAT THESE FACTS:

- **As referenced earlier, within the next 10 years, three million more women than men will be enrolled in college.**

- **At that time, the hiring population will be mostly female.**

HELLO! GET THE PICTURE?
WOMEN ARE TAKING OVER!

They are moving up and out, and they're moving in. Men who are uncomfortable with educated, smart, sharp, financially astute women in authoritative roles are going to have serious issues. They need to begin to change how they think about women. In order for businesses to grow, managers and executives need to make sure their organizations have brilliant women in the boardrooms so they stay in tune with the significant economic and labor power that women now have and will have in the future.

According to a comprehensive study by McKinsey + Company, in partnership with LeanIn.Org: "A year and a half into the COVID-19 pandemic, women in corporate America are even more burned out than they were last year – more so than men. Despite this added stress and exhaustion, women are rising to the moment as stronger leaders and taking on the extra work that comes with this: compared with men at the same level, women are doing more to support their teams and advance diversity, equity, and inclusion efforts. They are also more likely to be allies to women of color."

When I read that, I was saying, "YES! YES!"

The report goes on to say, "The path forward is clear. Companies need to take bold steps to address burnout. They need to recognize and reward the women leaders who are driving progress. And they need to do the deep cultural work required to create a workplace where all women feel valued" (Special Report, "Women in the Workplace 2021," September 27, 2021).

RECOMMENDATION

If business owners and executives really want to ignite the power of the women they are working with, then consider these actions:

- **When you hire a woman, be intentional about pairing her with an ambassador who acts as a buddy for her.** This should be someone who will be able to show her the lay of the land, make introductions, 15-minute meet-and-greets. This ensures that she will be able to gain footing in a new place and creates stickiness. Make sure this mentor helps her build connections and networks. Make sure this person opens doors for her.

- **Give the women in your organization an opportunity to "test drive" leadership roles.** If they are comfortable, engaged and effective in these temporary positions, then by all means, open the doors for them to assume these roles permanently. Promote these women early and often.

- **Men, decide to be an ally to women.** Speak up if you notice male colleagues behaving micro-aggressively, such as making subtle comments expressing a prejudiced attitude, such as *That woman is not fit for this job and should go home, bake cookies and take care of her children.* Refrain from marginalizing or minimizing what a woman says. Champion her ideas and celebrate her strengths. Leave the good ol' boys club behind. It's closed anyway.

- **Create a flexible workplace where women with fragile support networks can still earn a viable income.**

- **Create an internal development program for women to connect them with an executive coach or a peer cohort.** This is not my idea. I must give credit to Jessica Hendrickson, a Fortune 500 executive, and Dr. Chris Sopa. They invited me to be one of the coaches for twenty-four brilliant female executives in Fortune 500 companies. As the token male, I learned more from them than I think they learned from me.

- **Sadly, what I have seen more often than women embracing and engaging their own remarkable talents in the workplace are females trying to act like males.** Somewhere along the way, women bought into the myth that in order to be successful, they have to play like the men and abide by the rules of engagement men have established. So, the very attributes and skills that make women invaluable to their companies get pushed down and locked away.

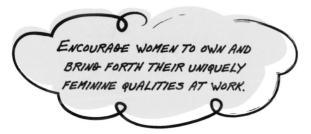

ENCOURAGE WOMEN TO OWN AND BRING FORTH THEIR UNIQUELY FEMININE QUALITIES AT WORK.

- **Ask them to offer their perspectives on business matters.** Ask about their intuition, their sixth sense, about the people you're doing business with. Challenge a female colleague intellectually and watch what happens. She will step up like never before if given the opportunity.

- **It's unjust, but still today, women aren't paid on the same level as their male counterparts. Don't accept this!** If you're a small-business owner, it has to start with you. After all, you're the backbone of this country, the most nimble and flexible of companies around. You're the ones who can respond to and move quickly on issues like pay equity. The bottom line for igniting the power of women in business is to pay them fairly.

- **When you conduct business with women, and I encourage you to do just that, treat each of them as if they are your blood sisters.**

- **If you're married to or dating a working woman, be her sounding board.** Listen closely, but don't offer to fix anything for her unless she asks you to.

WOMEN,
IF YOU'RE READING THIS...

I'd like to talk to you about the many ways you can prove your worth within your corporation and experience greater success as well:

1. **First of all, women need to find and exude confidence.** I'm not talking about swagger, posturing, political gamesmanship or artificial confidence. I'm talking about quiet confidence that has to do with you knowing your passions and pursuing them relentlessly. Forget climbing the corporate ladder. Instead, connect with people, be accountable for yourself in every way and commit to being a part of the solution.

2. **Secondly, find a mentor, someone who "gets you."** I'm not talking here about an executive coach, someone who wants to play it safe with your feelings. I'm talking about someone who knows you well and who has the guts to tell you if you're not cutting it, why you're not cutting it and what is holding you back.

3. **Develop a strategic career plan that charts what you want to accomplish and where you want to be in one year, three years, five years.** Begin to act as if everything is possible. Believe that you can drive value, make a difference and take your team or company to the next level.

4. **Women who seek to gain respect and equal footing in the marketplace should sit down with their managing directors and leaders and have a conversation about working styles, rules of engagement, ideal work environments and simply what makes them and other managers tick.** Attention to that level of detail will ensure clarity, understanding and cooperation in your professional relationships.

EPILOGUE

I hope this book has challenged and called you to do better and be better as the men in our women's lives. While many of us get distracted by our wives' or our girlfriends' pretty female wrapping and their nice feminine trappings, I hope I've encouraged you to look deeper and discover who they really are, what moves them, what energizes them, what saddens them, what they love, how to honor them, and teach our sons to do the same. There is not just a stream but a floodgate of power that lies waiting to be unleashed in the women we love and work with, and thereby in our own selves. Are you ready to take your rightful place as a conduit, an igniter and a sparkler?

> YES, THIS IS THE AGE OF THE WOMAN AND, YES, THEY ARE AND WILL CONTINUE TO BE A FORCE TO BE RECKONED WITH.

But guess what? They need us as much as we need them. And in order to live together in the most triumphant, productive and kindhearted way, we men must learn to stoke the fires within their hearts and minds and then bask in its comforting heat. So, let's be intentional about igniting the power of the women in our lives.

ABOUT THE AUTHOR

SIMON'S PURPOSE IS TO
➤➤ SPARK LISTENERS ⬅⬅
TO LEAD COUNTRIES, COMPANIES,
AND COMMUNITIES DIFFERENTLY.

His framework is based on his 30 years' of experience in the hospitality industry, including serving as sales director for Disney Institute, based at Walt Disney World Resort in Orlando, FL. He is a prolific author and Hall of Fame Keynote Speaker that has worked with Signet Jewelers, SalesForce, T-Mobile, Stanford Healthcare, General Mills and Hilton Hotels just to name a few.

AN EXPERIENCE WITH SIMON GOES BEYOND FEEL-GOOD CONTENT.

HE DELIVERS PRACTICAL STRATEGIES AND
IMPACTS REAL LIVES.

He connects with any audience on many levels with a relevant message that resonates beyond the stage.

Simon's viral video posted by Goalcast to Facebook has over 90 million views and LinkedIn Learning features three of his online courses that reach professionals in 100 countries. Recently, Simon became a certified Caritas Coach, leading with heart-centered intelligence. His approach is grounded in Caring Science that focuses on preserving human dignity, wholeness as the highest gift to self, systems, and society.

His wisdom and expertise enabled an Orlando-based healthcare system to be acquired and a division of a hospitality company to be ranked No. 1 for customer service by Expedia.com. Simon serves on two unique boards; U.S. Dream Academy and Orlando Health Foundation where he is a five year board member that has 20,000 employees and over $1 Billion in revenue. Recently, Cleary University, a 138 year old institution in Holland, Michigan, rewarded him with a Doctorate of Science in Business Administration for his global impact.

BOOKS & EBOOKS
BY SIMON T. BAILEY

- **Be The Spark:** *Five Platinum Service Principles for Creating Customers for Life*

- **Success is an Inside Job** with bonus book **Brilliant Service is the Bottom Line**

- **Release Your Brilliance:** *The 4 Steps to Transforming Your Life and Revealing Your Genius to the World* (also available in Spanish and Portuguese)

- **Shift Your Brilliance:** *Harness the Power of You, Inc.*

- **Brilliant Living:** *31 Insights to Creating an Awesome Life*

- **Releasing Leadership Brilliance:** *Breaking Sound Barriers in Education* co-written with Dr. Marceta F. Reilly

- **Meditate on Your Personal Brilliance**

- **Meditate on Your Professional Brilliance**

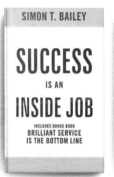

SELF-PACED COURSES & TRAINING PROGRAMS

BY SIMON T. BAILEY

- **Shift Your Brilliance System**

  Become your best self. Shift Your Brilliance helps you direct your own personal development narrative. You'll learn how to become a leader of the future and Chief Breakthrough Officer of your organization.

- **Brilliant Presenter**

  Everyone wants to be a speaker. Whether it's in the boardroom, to your family, or in front of 10,000 people, this course will teach you how to speak effectively. Give a brilliant presentation and watch the new clients, promotions, opportunities, and life changes start to roll in. Your life and career will be forever transformed.

- **Shift to Brilliance**

  This course will give you twelve ways to jumpstart your business, career, and life.

- **Building Business Relationships**

  There are four key types of business relationships in your career: your manager, your coworkers, other departments, and executives. In this LinkedIn Learning Course, Simon is your guide to building authentic connections with others to create your own personal board of directors for success.

- **Finding a Sponsor**

  The workforce may be competitive, but you are not alone. The individuals who see your ambition and point you in the right direction can act as advocates. In this best-selling LinkedIn Learning Course. Simon helps you build a trusting relationship with a sponsor – and change the course of your career.

All books, eBooks, coaching programs, courses and more are available at www.simontbailey.com

CONNECT
WITH SIMON T. BAILEY

To Purchase Bulk Copies of *Ignite the Power of Women in Your Life:*
hello@simontbailey.com
407-970-1113

 Sign up for our free weekly newsletter and free digital gift:
www.simontbailey.com

 Simon's blog:
www.simontbailey.com/blog/

 Follow Simon:
https://www.instagram.com/simontbailey/

 Listen to Simon:
https://www.youtube.com/c/SimonTBaileyIntl

 Link with Simon:
www.linkedin.com/in/simontbailey

 Book Simon to Speak at Your Event:
hello@simontbailey.com
407-970-1113

CPSIA information can be obtained
at www.ICGtesting.com
Printed in the USA
BVHW020427290722
643302BV00002B/6